TRUE CRIME STORIES
OF
BURLINGTON, VERMONT

TRUE CRIME STORIES
OF
BURLINGTON, VERMONT

THEA LEWIS

THE
History
PRESS

Published by The History Press
Charleston, SC
www.historypress.com

First published 2023

Manufactured in the United States

ISBN 9781467154451

Library of Congress Control Number: 2023937208

Notice: The information in this book is true and complete to the best of our knowledge. It is offered without guarantee on the part of the author or The History Press. The author and The History Press disclaim all liability in connection with the use of this book.

CONTENTS

CONTENTS

PREFACE

Mrs. Dorothy O'Leary, a mother of five, was charged with making five liquor sales illegally. When her place was raided by enforcement officers, a quantity of liquor was seized. Upon her willingness to plead guilty, State's Attorney Clarke A. Gravel nolle prossed four of the charges of selling. Judge Willsie E. Brisbin sentenced her to serve 90 days in the county jail and then suspended her sentence, and placed her on probation until further order of the court. She will pay court costs of about $12.00. She also waived her right to the liquor which was seized from her.

—Burlington Free Press, *November 26, 1946*

Before writing this book, I thought long and hard about how to present the stories and characters other books and movies might call "ripped from the headlines." My research into many of the stories that follow were certainly headline fodder, some dating to long before I was born. Some I was familiar with through research I'd done for my true crime tours. But others are personal, because even though I've never been charged with a major crime (in fact, I've never even gotten a speeding ticket), I have existed at the fringes of crimes committed by people I know, some only in passing and, some, very, very well.

The preceding excerpt taken from the *Burlington Free Press* is one example of these stories. For decades, I was ignorant of the incident that has become, for me, family lore.

Some years ago, I was writing a book called *Wicked Vermont*. While falling down the rabbit hole of vintage newspapers, searching for quirky Vermont stories, I came across a familiar name: Dorothy O'Leary, busted for selling hooch out her back door, was my maternal grandmother.

Reading about her arrest, I was shocked. I called my mother and asked, "Did you know about this?" She laughed and said of course she'd known. Then she told me the whole story.

My grandmother, a single mother with a lot to deal with, was a "bootstrap" kind of gal. There wasn't a thing she couldn't do if she put her mind to it. A seamstress by trade, she was organized and had a head for money, so in those days, when residents of Battery Street looked out for one another and shared their individual talents, she was the neighborhood "banker," holding on to their cash until they needed it.

Usually working more than one job with five small mouths to feed, she figured out a way to make a little extra money on the side: selling liquor on the down-low on Sundays, when Vermont's Blue Laws decreed bars were closed.

One day, she and her younger sister, Doris, were talking in the kitchen when there was a knock at the front door. She went to answer it, and Doris trailed after her. Outside was a tall, dark, well-groomed and well-dressed man. He said he was there to buy "a shot." My grandmother said "Sure," and instructed him to go to the back door. As she hurried to grab the bottle to give the guy what he wanted, Doris said, "You're not going to sell to him, are you, Dot? We don't know him!"

My grandmother laughed and said, "Of course I am. Did you *see* him? He's gorgeous!"

She invited him in. She poured a shot. He handed her the money.

As soon as her fist closed around the cash, the back and front doors of her apartment burst open, and men from liquor control swarmed into the apartment to search rooms, go through drawers and, most upsetting to my mother, who was just a little kid at the time, rifle through bags of small Christmas gifts she'd just bought downtown.

Dumbfounded at hearing all this, I told my mother, "I can't believe you never mentioned this." She said, "I thought you knew."

Technically, Burlington, Vermont, is a city, but in a lot of ways, especially in the Old North End, where I grew up, it can feel like a small town. I've been privy to some pretty wild and illicit shenanigans, simply because I knew someone who knew someone.

Writing this book has been captivating, haunting and cathartic in ways I never expected. It's also been an eye-opening look at how Vermont criminals and victims have, historically, been treated and portrayed.

I hope you enjoy it.

ACKNOWLEDGEMENTS

B ooks don't write themselves, and authors, however skilled, don't write them alone. This particular book would never have made it to the page without backup from my own "partners in crime," people who acted as sounding boards, provided technical expertise, kept me sane and pulled off some last-minute miracles.

I want to thank my husband, Roger Lewis (as his online French lessons would say, the man is nonpareil) for his eagle eye, his jokes when the going got tough and for picking up the slack of daily life.

I'm also grateful to my kids, Shannon Redmond and Kylie Richards, who somehow managed to come up with a motivating phrase via return text whenever I would whine.

Special recognition is due my sister Lee Anne Billings, who was a wealth of information and an unflagging cheerleader through some of the hardest months of her life, and former Chittenden County state's attorney Mark Keller, who provided clarity and some priceless true crime tidbits from the repository of his steel trap mind.

I'm especially indebted to Diane Landry, who was an eleventh-hour finder of ancient photographic artifacts, and Mike Kinsella and the rest of the team at The History Press, who provided such invaluable support throughout.

Relatives and friends—too numerous to mention—helped without even knowing it through their interest and enthusiasm. I appreciate them all.

Finally, many thanks to the late Marselis Parsons, a journalist whose insight, wit and knack for storytelling helped make me a better writer.

1

THE CASE OF
THE BOOK-LOVING BUTCHER

Israel Freeman, a Black veteran of the Civil War who'd served with the Fifty-Fourth Massachusetts Regiment, was a complicated man. His superiors during the Civil War thought his career in the armed forces could have been distinguished, since he was as bright as he was brave. Unfortunately, he had a highly emotional nature that included a hair-trigger temper when he was drunk, which was often. Known for a general recklessness with weapons whenever he was excited, he was notorious for drawing knives on men during fights.

In May 1863, he was taken to court for disorderly conduct after threatening two enlisted men, offering to "relieve them of their heads by knocking them off." He was fined five dollars.

At the beginning of January 1864, the *Burlington Free Press* noted, "Freeman, one of the Massachusetts 54th regiment in the civil war notoriously celebrated a Happy New Year on Water Street. Charged with resisting an officer and fined $10."

In November 1868, he was charged again, this time with being drunk and belligerent at a local dance hall. The next year, he and a Monkton, Vermont man named Kevin Mulaney were each fined five dollars for public intoxication and disorderly conduct for fighting with each other. The two later testified they had purchased a quart of alcohol at a drugstore to apply to a lame horse but had ended up drinking it instead. (There was no word on how the horse made out.)

Burlington Waterfront circa 1870. *University of Vermont Libraries.*

On October 26, 1871, Freeman was in his room in a multifamily house on the corner of Burlington's Cherry and Water Streets (known as Battery Street today) that he shared with his mother, Clarissa, and a boarder, twenty-three-year-old William Carbo.

Freeman worked as a butcher postwar, and one of his recreational pursuits was collecting and reading dime novels, inexpensive, sensational tales that were often sold for less than ten cents. Back in the 1800s, they usually featured stories of heroic and adventurous characters in the form of soldiers, "Indian fighters," detectives or frontiersmen. They were the paperback books of their day, and Freeman owned quite a few.

William Carbo was a local boy, the result of an unfortunate and chaotic upbringing, with no father in the picture and a mother who, due to her impoverishment, was forced to place some of her brood with the city's Home for Destitute Children. Carbo would often assist Freeman on his butchering jobs, so they were together much of the time.

On October 26, 1871, between three and four o'clock in the afternoon, Freeman and Carbo were in their second-floor rooms, looking at a new book Freeman had just added to his collection, when a friend of Freeman, a man named John Hallahan, passed by on the street below. Freeman called to him from the window, telling him to come up to see his books.

There was a pail of beer in the room, and it was evident to Hallahan the two men had been drinking, but it seemed Freeman was the only one who was drunk. Sometime during the course of their conversation, Freeman realized his brand-new book was missing, and he asked Carbo where it was. Carbo denied having it. That's when Freeman called him a "son of a bitch" and a "goddamn liar." He swore he would "fix" Carbo, and young William, in what I think may have been an unfortunate miscalculation of the situation, told Freeman, "You've threatened me before." That's when the butcher made for his basket of tools. Carbo grabbed at the larger man to restrain him, and when he did this, Freeman punched him in the eye. A scuffle ensued, and the older man tripped, ending up face-down on the floor, his bag of butchering knives mere inches from his reach. Carbo, crouching over him, saw his one chance for survival. He held Freeman's neck and reached for the heavy hatchet on top of the basket of tools. Grasping the handle, he struck two deadly blows, splitting Freeman's head from back to front. The butcher's brains fell out onto the floor.

Hallahan, sickened by the sight, ran down the stairs and up the street, spreading the news as he ran. Carbo ran, too, to City Hall, mere blocks away, to find Officer White, the man in charge of the city jail.

When he got there, he burst into tears. "I have killed Israel Freeman. I want you to take me to jail," he cried. The officer did as he asked.

Neighbors who Hallahan had alerted rushed into Freeman's house and found him lying in a pool of blood. A local physician, Dr. Crandall, was called but immediately saw Freeman was beyond the point at which he or

Burlington's old city hall. *University of Vermont Libraries, Special Collections.*

his black bag could be of any use. Mr. Lowry, the superintendent of the poor was sent for and came to claim Freeman's corpse.

Carbo was arraigned the next day in front of a large and curious crowd. Local papers speculated that he would likely not be charged with "murder in the first" but said a second-degree murder charge could still mean a long prison sentence.

Unable to post bail, Carbo remained locked up for nearly a year. Justice wasn't exactly swift. On September 26, 1872, he was finally tried and found not guilty by reason of self-defense.

Carbo lost a year of freedom and likely learned every trick in the book from all the criminals, petty or otherwise, he encountered while in the pokey. Later articles in the local news feature him charged with everything from burglary and being an informant to disturbing the peace at local bawdy houses.

2

THE HABITS OF
LOCAL NIGHT BIRDS

Boys will be boys, the saying goes, especially on a Saturday night in 1881 in one of the roughest parts of Burlington. During the late 1800s, Battery Street, covered with tenements, lumberyards, factories, inns and stores, bustled in broad daylight. It was a place with a reputation, where, after dark, locals and visitors might drift about in the shadows, looking for illicit entertainment. This could be found at one of the area's numerous houses of ill-fame, but there were also simpler, cheaper pleasures, like gambling or sharing a pail of beer at a business that was willing to receive guests after closing time.

It's hard to imagine the particular wildness that comes over a Vermonter in late April, when the cold weather breaks, the trees begin to bud and you're looking down the barrel of mud season into the heat of summer. It's a feeling I know well, and I imagine there was plenty of this feeling in the air the night Frank McCullough, part of a fun-loving young group of Irishmen looking for diversion, was disemboweled at a local lumberyard.

A *Burlington Free Press* headline that read, "The Habits of Local Night Birds," told how two parties of young men met up at Lavigne's Grocery on Battery Street when a Frenchman, Albert Mercier, prompted by Lavigne himself, attempted to cut short the merrymaking. Then an Irishman named McCullough and his cohorts caused trouble.

If you believe the initial reports, the Irishmen mentioned were already three sheets to the wind when twenty-four-year-old Frank and his sixteen-year-old brother, Isidore, arrived at Lavigne's with their friend Paul Viens in tow. But look again and read some more, because news stories from back in the day weren't always what they were cracked up to be. Those poor ink-stained wretches in the newsroom weren't held to the journalistic standards reporters are held to today. Their accounts were often biased and their comments condescending. On occasion, slurs were used outright.

In this case, to be fair, the local police seemed to lean heavily on first impressions. The paper may have simply followed their lead, using the simplest and most condensed version of the story. But as time went by, more pieces of the patchwork quilt of events became available, and it looks like the incident went down like this:

Frank McCullough, Dennis Nash, Daniel Sullivan, Fardee Clorin, Thomas Fassett and Charles Farmer, friends of the grocer Lavigne, were inside his place of business, shooting craps, when Mercier, who'd emigrated from Quebec's Eastern Townships the year before and was employed as an assistant engineer at a local mill, showed up with Isidore and Paul. He was looking for beer and was told by the group there was none (no doubt, they were lying). He began to encourage them to go up the street with him, where there was plenty of beer available for a price. The Irish boys, some of whom had already been drinking, were content among themselves, shooting craps for peanuts (yes, actual peanuts), so they declined, and Mercier and his two cohorts left the store.

They returned a bit later, and Lavigne, who, meanwhile, had managed to find a bucket of beer, told them they had to go. They did but objected that the Irishmen weren't also hustled off the premises. A slur was uttered. Mercier said the slur was muttered by the Irish about the French. The Irish said the slur was uttered by Mercier about the Irish. There was a rumble inside the grocery. Someone knocked over the store's coal stove.

Mercier and his boys ended up outside, pushing at the door, trying to get back in. A punch was thrown, and the lot of them ended up on the street, where they began throwing rocks at each other. Mercier hit McCullough with a rock, and McCullough, pissed in more ways than one, set after him. Mercier began to run, McCullough not far behind and Fassett his close second.

Mercier claimed that while he ran, he had no presence of mind regarding the fate of his brother or his friend, saying he headed to the north side of the Shepard and Morse Lumber Company sheds, through the train depot and up to College Street. He said that when he got there, he heard someone had been hurt in the fight and worried it was his brother. He returned to Lavigne's, he said, but Isidore wasn't there. He was safe with their mother,

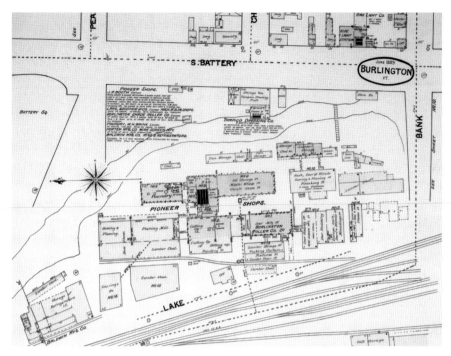

Sanborn map detail, pioneer shops. *University of Vermont Libraries, Special Collections.*

who lived directly across from the grocer's store. Mercier said after he found his brother, he walked to his own house, mere blocks away on Front Street, and went to bed.

Common sense would tell you Mercier's story left a few things out.

Frank McCullough's version of the story was, in light of the events leading up to it, more believable. He said he was hit with a rock by Albert Mercier, after which he and Fassett chased after him on the dark streets of Burlington's waterfront. But, he said, when they got to the retail shops, Mercier suddenly changed direction, a ruse. As McCullough approached him, the younger man wheeled about and, with an underhand blow of his knife, caught McCullough in the abdomen, creating a two-inch slice that allowed about two feet of McCullough's intestines to spill out of his abdominal cavity.

It is known that McCullough was half-carried by Fassett to a nearby house at the corner of Battery and Bank Streets, where the resident refused to let them inside. Frank McCullough languished on the doorstep until Patrick Griffin, an adjoining neighbor and off-duty policeman, woke up and brought the men inside his home. A doctor was sent for, and transportation was arranged. McCullough, taken to the Mary Fletcher Hospital on Colchester

Avenue, was in dire straits. He was given drugs and made as comfortable as possible, but Dr. Leroy Bingham, who attended him, knew that fecal matter had leaked into the man's tissues, peritonitis was likely setting in and the prognosis wasn't good.

When the police arrived at Mercier's Front Street home, he denied causing the injury, even claiming he was never in possession of a knife. Apparently, he was so convincing, he had police scratching their heads. *Somebody* stabbed McCullough. But Mercier had no criminal record that they knew of, and as the newspaper later comically pointed out, the young man didn't *look* like a killer. Was McCullough stabbed, not by Mercier, but during the mêlée outside Lavigne's? But they wondered how that could make sense. Mercier claimed he'd been *chased* by McCullough. In their minds, it would have been nearly impossible for someone with such a serious wound—basically disemboweled—to pursue the Frenchman even a short distance. They jailed Mercier—with reservations.

Burlington in the late 1800s was a heavily French Canadian community. This was also a time when the Irish in America were not well-regarded. So, if a fight of any consequence was going to break out between a gaggle of Irishmen and a cluster of Frenchmen, it's a pretty sure bet the authorities would find the Irish were to blame. And McCullough already had strikes against him. The twenty-eight-year-old unmarried lumberyard worker was a rowdy fellow and a regular in court for his many misdemeanors. As a younger man, he had even served time in prison. His companions were also in the habit of breaking the law.

Left: Mary Fletcher Hospital. *University of Vermont Libraries, Special Collections.*

Opposite: R. Bunting and Son Sheffield Folding Dirk. *Private collection.*

Speaking of McCullough's rough-around-the-edges pals, they were questioned, but most were tight-lipped, leaving police to sift through what little they did say to try to uncover the truth.

Meanwhile, at the hospital, there wasn't much to do but wait. Doctors gave McCullough about twenty-four hours, if he was lucky, to get right with his loved ones, himself and his maker. Father O'Sullivan of St. Mary's Cathedral administered last rites. In front of the priest and McCullough's sister, Frank told the officers who were questioning him that he had forgiven Mercier for stabbing him, worrying they shouldn't "do anything to him." "We'll tend to that ourselves," Sheriff Drew assured him as they took the dying man's final deposition. His desperate state and his charity toward Mercier aside, McCullough's story about the events of the previous evening never changed. It's worth mentioning he was concerned his testimony might incriminate Lavigne (for violating liquor laws by letting them drink in his establishment in the first place).

At 2:10 a.m., twenty-six hours after he was stabbed, Frank McCullough died.

When Albert Mercier was arraigned the next day, he seemed mostly unconcerned. It's no wonder, since local papers made note that while he was sitting in the courtroom, looking just a bit nervous, Mercier could never be pegged as a criminal. The guy must have had the face of a cherub.

But when it came time for Mercier's trial, it was apparent the Frenchman hadn't told the truth. A basic knowledge of human nature, a familiarity with Burlington's geography, an inkling of the limitations of the human body and, most importantly, witness testimony led most to believe the man deserved at least a charge of manslaughter. Sheriff Drew and Officer Price said Mercier repeatedly claimed he could not have stabbed McCullough because he didn't have a knife, but aside from that, his story didn't make sense. And on top of that, the prosecution brought forth a witness, a man who worked with Mercier, Charles Hurley, who had, in fact, borrowed from Mercier a black-handled dagger with a five-inch blade called a Dirk knife that he'd returned to him the day of the murder. Hurley's testimony

was supported by several other men who had seen Mercier using such a knife.

In the end, blade or no blade, liar or not, Albert Mercier was found not guilty, because the jury ruled he acted in self-defense. Perhaps they'd read it in one of the local papers, which had come to the following conclusion before the verdict was handed down:

> *At worst it was only a case of manslaughter, and it would be difficult, it seems to us, to make any ordinary jury consider it other than an act of self-defense, as the Frenchman was in full flight, was overtaken, and had he not used his knife would have been terribly beaten, perhaps killed.*

3

UVM'S DEADLIEST STUDENT

The University of Vermont in Burlington's Hill Section is no stranger to notoriety. In 1987, *Playboy* magazine named it number four on its list of the top forty "party colleges" in the United States. John Dewey, the father of modern education, is a noted alumnus, as is author Annie Proulx. The actor Ben Affleck, though he graduated elsewhere, is also a noted former student. UVM even spawned the popular band Phish. But there's one student in UVM's long history who is recalled not for his accolades but for his crimes—his many, many crimes. That man, Herman Webster Mudgett, is better known as H.H. Holmes, America's first serial killer.

H.H. Holmes was born in 1860 in the town of Gilmantown, New Hampshire. Herman's father, a devout Methodist who held the position as the town's postmaster, was said to be a strict disciplinarian. Depending on what you read, he was either a "spare the rod, spoil the child" type or a vicious sadist who beat Herman often.

Reports of Holmes's early years often note the boy was close to his mother, spending a great deal of time with her at the family home, likely reading Jules Verne or Edgar Allen Poe. Holmes was absolutely a loner, and his only friend died from a fall. (Are you suspicious? It would be hard not to be.)

Herman was a bright boy, likely a genius, fascinated with creating inventions and terrified of death—though, unfortunately for the over two hundred people he may have killed in his lifetime, he did get over his repulsion. This may have occurred when a group of local boys found out there was a cadaver at the town doctor's office and forced Herman to view the skeletal

Left: The murderer H.H. Holmes. *Public domain.*

Right: A young H.H. Holmes. *Public domain.*

remains. Later in life, Holmes revealed that rather than being overwhelmed with dread by the corpse, he was completely fascinated—enough to begin capturing small animals so he could conduct "experiments" on them.

At the age of sixteen, Holmes graduated from New Hampshire's historic Phillips Exeter Academy, and much to my horror, he had an early career as a teacher.

On July 4, 1878, he eloped with a sweet-faced girl named Clara Lovering, a young woman from a well-to-do family whose father was a member of New Hampshire's state legislature. He left teaching for a while and took up work as a clerk in Concord, New Hampshire, and on February 3, 1880, Clara gave birth to their son, Robert Lovering Mudgett.

With a talent for dissection already under his belt, Holmes decided he would attend medical school at the University of Vermont. Clara agreed to support him using whatever marketable talents she had, likely sewing or mending. He enrolled at the age of eighteen and lasted at the school only one year. He left, saying the place was too small to suit his needs. If you ask me, the city of Burlington was too closely knit, too much a place where everyone knew everyone else's business, for him to feel comfortable, despite the financial opportunities it presented.

This is largely speculation, but the city's waterfront back then was bustling by day and dangerously dark at night. It was the perfect place for Holmes to obtain the cadavers local doctors and medical students needed. In those days, a dead body procured for research purposes would cost about thirty dollars, and later in his life, suspected of murder, Holmes

Holmes's first wife, Clara Lovering. *Public domain.*

did admit to grave-digging and using medical cadavers to defraud insurance companies—a grisly way to fatten one's pocketbook.

Bidding Burlington farewell, Holmes transferred to the University of Michigan. This time, Clara joined him, but theirs was not a happy marriage; in fact, it was filled with violence. In 1884, after his knocking her around escalated to near-fatal fights, Clara took their son and moved back to New Hampshire.

Holmes graduated and moved to Mooers Forks, New York, to take a position as a school principal. His time there was apparently quite eventful. A small boy who was last seen with "Master Holmes" went missing. The wife of a couple he was boarding with, with whom he'd been dallying, became pregnant, and Holmes didn't want to stick around to see who the little stranger looked like. He skipped town in the middle of the night to avoid paying the rent he owed and possible violence.

Off he went to Philadelphia, Pennsylvania, where he secured work at a drugstore. When a young boy died after taking a medication Holmes had given him, Holmes played it off as an accident and left the city.

While he was still married to Clara, Holmes married a woman named Myrta Belknap, adding bigamy to his list of transgressions. He moved with his new wife to Chicago. It was there that he left his old identity, Herman Mudgett, behind completely, registering in that city as H.H. Holmes.

Devious but charming and handsome with what today might be called a "fireman's mustache," Holmes had a way with women. In Chicago, he convinced a pharmacy owner, Dr. Elizabeth Holton, to give him a job. Those familiar with Holmes's story will note that previous accounts have indicated Holton and her husband were an elderly couple, a pharmacist and his *wife*, duped by and killed by Holmes; however, recent research has brought to light that Dr. Holton was, in fact, a woman who was only a little older than Holmes with a husband who held various jobs.

For whatever reason, perhaps overburdened with the responsibilities of being a wife, mother and business owner, Holton sold her business to Holmes. There is every indication that he never paid her the amount they agreed on, just part of a pattern of not living up to his financial obligations that followed Holmes most of his life. He wasn't great at matrimonial obligations either. Myrta Belknap, who wouldn't tolerate Holmes's wandering eye, left him and went back to live with her parents.

With that relationship resolved, Holmes turned his attention to the two things he liked most: killing and real estate. He began constructing the hotel that would one day become Chicago's Murder Castle, or the Castle of Horrors.

Designed completely by the evil mastermind, the hotel was filled with so many twists and opportunistically dark hiding places, even the contractors he hired didn't know the true layout of the place. The castle contained seventy-one guest rooms on its second and third floors that could be locked only from the outside. Each was fitted with a gas valve connected to a control panel in Holmes's room, so guests could be done away with in the middle of the night. Once Holmes had a victim in his clutches, disposal of evidence wasn't hard. Greased shoots fed directly to the basement, where he kept a dissecting table, an acid tank and a crematorium.

Holmes hired a man named Ned Connor to run a jewelry store on the hotel's first floor. Ned was a friendly fellow with an attractive wife named Julia, who was nearly six feet tall, which, for a woman back then, was noteworthy. Holmes fell for her and vice versa, and she soon discovered she was pregnant. He talked her into letting him perform an abortion in his lab. Not long afterward, he paid an employee to transport a skeleton to a local medical college. The doctor who received it was keen to have it, because it was such an unusual specimen—imagine, a female skeleton measuring six feet in height.

With the Chicago World's Fair happening just a few blocks from his castle, Holmes's murderous antics grew to reach a much larger scale. In those days of few phones and no email or social media, it was easy to lose someone, especially if they'd been found by Holmes first.

Holmes would sometimes convince young people he met at the fair to take positions in the various businesses located in the retail portion of his castle under the condition that they take out insurance policies that named him as the beneficiary.

In the mid-1990s, Holmes, a serial bigamist, wed two different women. One of these women was Miss Minnie Williams, an actress he met in Boston, where he was traveling under an assumed name. Minnie moved to Chicago to be Holmes's secretary, and he discovered her father, a doctor, had died in her youth, leaving her and her sister, Nannie, money and property that he was keen to cash in. Not long after they were married, Minnie died by poisoning, never knowing Holmes had already killed her sister, Nannie. He met Nannie at the train before marrying Minnie and took her to the hotel, where he left her to suffocate in an airtight vault.

The 1893 Chicago World's Fair. *Library of Congress Archives.*

Holmes, while traveling to the Fort Worth area to collect the girls' fortune, pulled various moneymaking cons, including horse theft, under three different aliases.

Young Georgiana Yoke was working as a clerk in a Chicago department store when she met Holmes. He married her in what was his second marriage in a less than a year. Like his other wives, she was unaware he was a con man, kidnapper and murderer, and she may have never discovered his cons if he hadn't relied on the dead man's shuffle.

Dead man's shuffle was a bold insurance scam, and for Holmes, it was a major moneymaking scheme. In it, an insurance policy would be taken out on an individual, and later, someone else's dead body, a reasonable facsimile, would be presented as the corpse. Holmes did this in 1894 with Benjamin Pitezel, who was working as the manager of his boardinghouse. In need of cash, Pitezel took out an insurance policy on himself in the amount of $10,000, with Holmes cut into the deal. All they needed was a look-alike corpse. Instead, Holmes killed his employee, telling Pitezel's wife, Carrie, that her husband had flown the coop.

Left: Benjamin Pitezel. *Public domain.*

Right: Patrolman David S. Richards assisted in tracking Holmes. *Public domain.*

After bumping off Ben Pitezel, Holmes fed Carrie falsehoods about the whereabouts of her husband and her children, whom he'd taken to ensure her silence. With them, he traveled the country to evade the investigators, who were hot on his trail, while traveling separately with Georgianna. It must have been quite a balancing act.

The three Pitezel children under Holmes's "care" met their ends by his hand. The charred remains of young Howard were found by Pinkerton agent Frank S. Geyer and Indiana detective David S. Richards in the stove of a house Holmes had occupied in Indiana. Nellie and Alice were discovered dead in the basement of an apartment Holmes had rented in Toronto. They had been buried with an implement Holmes had borrowed from a neighbor under the guise of planting potatoes.

The last stop for Carrie Pitezel during Holmes's "traveling show" was Burlington, his youthful stomping ground, a place far from Chicago. He was traveling using the name Truman Mudgett but sometimes switched to the surname Judson, just a few of his many aliases. He rented a furnished apartment for Carrie; her sixteen-year-old daughter, Meda; and her infant son at 26 North Winooski Avenue. Holmes stayed briefly on College Street at the Hotel Burlington to mind things but left within days for Boston.

Holmes now saw Carrie as nothing more than an inconvenience and a liability. She knew too much about the crimes he'd committed, and she knew what he was capable of. She was also suspicious of him—and rightly so. Unknown to her, while in Burlington, Holmes went to a local pharmacy and

26 North Winooski Avenue, Burlington, once home to Carrie Pitezel. *T. Lewis.*

purchased a bottle of nitro glycerine. He sent word to her to go down to the basement of the duplex to retrieve a bottle, telling her she should take it up to the attic. He gave particular instructions on where to find it and how to extract it. Carrie hesitated. She knew Holmes had been up to something in the basement, because she'd surprised him there, only to realize later what he'd been up to.

Fortunately, when she finally went to the basement, she started her search from the wrong direction, foiling the booby trap the killer had rigged, a trapdoor that was supposed to swing down and smash the bottle, causing it to explode. She buried the bottle beneath a window casement.

A desperate Carrie followed Holmes to Boston, where he was apprehended while trying to leave the country. His murder spree came to a close. Carrie was also arrested. In Burlington, Chief of Police Jerome Dumas searched the Greek Revival home on North Winooski Avenue, retrieving the bottle, now evidence, from the place Carrie described during questioning. The woman, who had suffered enough, was eventually set free.

Holmes's trial in Philadelphia and his subsequent execution by hanging were of great interest to residents of Burlington and a topic of much gossip and speculation in the Queen City.

The papers were filled with stories that stunned the nation but were a bit too close to home. They detailed Holmes's capture, his murderous exploits and the discovery of the remains of those he had killed—well, probably not *all* of them. He eventually confessed to twenty-seven murders, but it's thought there were many, many more.

Holmes was executed on May 7, 1896, in a public event at Philadelphia's Moyamensing Prison, where he had been incarcerated. After his execution, according to his wishes, his body was placed in a coffin that was filled with cement, buried and covered with another layer of cement to prevent anyone from exhuming his body to study his brain.

4

ALIAS, MOLLIE MATCHES

Famous thief and con artist John Larney, alias Mollie Matches, had something in common with Chester Arthur, the twenty-first president of the United States. Arthur, who was born in Vermont about a decade before Larney was born in Ireland, came from humble beginnings. He made up for it later in life, though, with a lavish lifestyle that included a love of fancy clothes. Arthur, the president whose mutton chop sideburns were the size of shower scrunchies, reportedly owned more than eighty pairs of trousers at a time and changed his pants *several times* a day.

According to those who knew and profiled Larney, possibly the most notorious pickpocket of the nineteenth century, he also had a weakness for fancy threads. Larney was also famously frugal. He didn't waste money on liquor, nor did he smoke; while he worked in no particular trade, he still managed to make real estate investments in Cleveland, Ohio, and various locations in Canada, because he also stole there.

Topping out at five feet, seven inches, and weighing 160 pounds, Larney usually sported a luxurious beard that hid a prominent chin dimple. His other distinguishing characteristics, should one get close enough to notice, included a small India ink mark on his left hand, between his thumb and forefinger, and a tattoo of part of an anchor on one arm. But then, getting half tattooed wasn't as serious or as lucrative as being a bounty jumper, which Larney was during the Civil War. Enlisting in Ohio, Pennsylvania, Massachusetts and New York, he collected the fees that were offered as enticements for soldiers to enlist and then skipped out without serving at all.

With his fine manners, elegant appearance and talent for observation, Larney was able to pull off many a ticklish heist. Silver-tongued when the con was on, he was often described as having the elocution of a preacher and the persuasiveness of a snake oil salesman. He was so good at conning people that during one prison sentence (he spent a good deal of his life incarcerated), he convinced his jailers he'd gone blind, resulting in his unsupervised use of the prison yard. He escaped, of course.

The infamous John Larney, alias "Mollie Matches." *From the* Chicago Daily News.

It was in July 1894, when Mollie Matches hit the streets of Vermont's Queen City. Residents innocently strolling Church Street or City Hall Park in the presence of the dapper stranger found themselves mysteriously relieved of their money and jewelry.

Larney, in Burlington, under the alias Dr. Denmark, preferred to board at the Hotel Van Ness on the corner of Main and St. Paul Streets, but in leaner times stayed at the boardinghouse owned by a partially deaf woman named Mrs. Hitchcock. His nine-to-five involved making the rounds of local stores, trolleys, restaurants, parks and the train station, picking people's pockets.

Mrs. Jeannette Shepardson of Fairfax was one of his victims. Leaving Burlington after a doctor's visit, she was standing on a train platform, wearing an eyepatch her doctor had applied, when the opportunistic Larney sidled up to stealthily claim her pocketbook.

Larney had seen the small city as a nice change of pace and easy pickings. But when Mrs. Shepardson made her complaint, the local constabulary caught on to Larney, who ran to a local barbershop to get rid of his beard to escape detection. It didn't work. The local police chief, Jerome Dumas, recognized that the thief who identified himself as Dr. George Hickock was indeed the infamous Mollie Matches.

In court, Chief Dumas testified that upon searching the belongings in Larney's room, he found a handful of coats that were believed to have belonged to the light-fingered felon. All their pockets were missing, and their linings were unhemmed. As the wolf in *Little Red Riding Hood* might say, "All the better to rob you with."

After a lengthy trial, Larney was convicted of theft and sentenced to serve three years in the Vermont State Prison in Windsor. Just five years later, John Larney made the papers in Montreal when he was caught picking the pockets of worshippers at the Church of the Holy Sacrament.

5

CALL HER MADAM

The earliest recorded mention of prostitution dates to circa 2400 BCE in ancient Samaria. The stigma surrounding "the oldest profession" has likely been around that long, too.

Vermont's Queen City has not been immune from illicit sexual shenanigans. A quick glance through newspaper archives reveal "street walkers" and "houses of ill-fame" were, for decades, of serious concern to the community and the constabulary.

Through the ages, even though prostitution has been largely frowned upon, some citizens were willing to turn a blind eye to how these soiled doves, as they were sometimes called, made their living, considering it a necessary evil.

To improve morale during the Civil War, some army officers encouraged the presence of prostitutes. In Nashville, U.S. brigadier general Robert S. Granger legalized sex for hire in an effort to curb the outbreak of venereal diseases among Union troops. The system implemented health checks and required ladies who were offering their services to be examined by a doctor at two-week intervals, for which they were charged a five-dollar registration fee and fifty cents per visit.

In Burlington's early days there were a vocal few who believed the solution to prostitution was not to eliminate it but regulate it. They, however, were in the minority. So, in the 1800s and into the 1900s, ladies of the night and their procurers played a game of cat and mouse with the local police. Many times, the cat won out, but sometimes, the mouse was smarter.

In the Queen City, as in other Vermont towns, when it came to where these women worked and for whom, a variety of situations came into play. Some grande horizontales (French for "great horizontals") fended for themselves, but many worked for bawdy houses and brothels.

A bawdy house was a place where people went for a bit of lower-class fun—the sex for hire equivalent of a dive bar. In the late 1800s, a Burlington woman named Fanny Borrette was infamous for her notorious house of ill repute at 166 Intervale Avenue in Burlington's Old North End, where brawls broke out nightly and visits from Sheriff Reeves and his officers were a regular occurrence. Many of Fanny's ladies spent long stints in prison, after which they were released and sent right back into the mayhem. One Sunday evening in October 1898, Fanny's bouncer Ed Howe fired his pistol during a raid by the local police and shot Thomas Hogan, who was said to be merely passing the venue.

Brothels were usually a bit more genteel, with work still regulated by a proprietor who, hopefully, had a better hand on the people working under them (pun intended). It usually saw a better-behaved clientele and sometimes—but not always—had a better relationship with local authorities. You could find girls (or boys) there and booze, along with other amusements.

Some prostitutes preferred to ply their trade solo. In 1909, a small-time strumpet named Georgianna Safford, whose stage name or alias was Margaret Spruce, made the local papers a few times for alleged acts of prostitution. After one incident involving the local police, she was fined $10.00 and court costs of $11.39. Not having the available funds, she served ninety days in jail. It's not known whether she was associated with a particular bawdy house or brothel, so it's possible she was self-employed.

In the columns of the *Burlington Free Press* or the *Burlington Daily News*, nobody captured interest quite like Philomene Lemoine.

Philomene Lemoine (also Pasha or Cathey), born in 1838, was an owner of brothels and a purveyor of girls and booze, and she was on the radar of the local police department for more than four decades. It didn't matter which last name she went by; people knew who she was.

From the 1870s to the early 1900s, her name was linked to prostitution in the Queen City more often than that of any other. With properties adjacent to Burlington's waterfront and in the city's French section of the Old North End, she had plenty of girls working for her and plenty of money coming from them.

In Philomene's heyday, she filled and refilled city coffers with the fines she paid. Cited into court again and again, she was often made to pay high bails

The Intervale Avenue home of Philomene Lemoine. *Roger Lewis.*

for her felonious activities. It probably comes as no surprise that vices like sex and liquor were big moneymakers not just for those who procured them but also for the legal system that passed judgement on their criminal activities.

At any rate, as madams go, Philomene seemed to have her act together. It's hard to know how she got started in the business—whether it was through opportunism or out of necessity. It's known she was a mother of two and that she cared for her own mother well into the woman's old age.

Philomene had "houses" on the corner of Battery and Main Streets and owned four separate parcels on Burlington's Intervale Avenue, a block that was just a stone's throw from the downtown area.

With those girls and others she "managed," she racked up one $300 bail charge after another. Busy woman that she was, the bails were often forfeited due to her failure to appear in court. She must have figured, "Why show up?" She was going to be fined anyway.

The largest sum recorded stemming from Philomene's court proceedings was a $10,000 bail charge, a huge amount of cash in those days, for what was essentially transporting a courtesan over state lines for immoral purposes. Two local men put up the cash. The case was eventually dismissed.

Not much is known about Philomene's personal relationships until the name George Cathey pops up.

Philomene married George, a younger man, later in life. Whether it was simply because their life goals and talents were a good match or because of some life crisis on her part is unclear, but George Cathey seemed more a cross to bear than a barrel of laughs.

He first turned up in 1900, when Philomene was in her early sixties. She bought him a fancy car, a 1908 Thomas touring car called a Red Devil. It had a six-cylinder engine and cost $6,000—that would be about $140,000 today. The car was wrecked while George and his chauffeur sped through the streets of Burlington but not before he was accused of handling the car in a manner that spooked the horses of Mrs. J.H. Dodds, the wife of a prominent local doctor, overturning her carriage and ruining her new outfit. She sued for damages.

George was also brought up on charges of trespassing and assault in a case initiated by a UVM student and sometime actor named Stanley F. White.

Example of a Thomas Touring car.
Library of Congress Archives.

36

White sought $300 in compensatory damages. The court granted $50. Philomene bought him a dog, a white-and-lemon-colored English setter. He lost it. Even with what little I know about life with George, I think it's likely the dog got smart and ran away.

George dropped out of the picture before 1910, after the sale of Philomene's Main Street property.

When Philomene died in January 1914, local papers mentioned that the poor, in particular, would miss her. It seems Philomene, during her time as Burlington's most audacious madam, also provided doctors' fees, money for burials and food baskets during the Christmas season. She was there when others' charity fell short. Like many a pop culture prostitute you read about in books and see in movies, she was "a hooker with a heart of gold."

She was buried without a marker in Burlington's Lakeview Cemetery.

6

WHAT THE @#!% DID YOU SAY?

W hat to think of May Bee, a brawler from Battery Street who hoped to become a bride?

Widowed a year from Samuel Bee, her second and most recent husband, she'd already made the local papers after he claimed she'd "pummeled" him. Police who responded to the home after he lodged the complaint said they heard language pass from the woman's lips that one did not usually expect from a lady.

Samuel dropped the charge but died in November 1918, eleven weeks after the assault, while battling Spanish influenza.

Not one to waste time, May became engaged to Fred Monette in October 1919 and would have made it to the altar except for a few outstanding warrants against her for breaching the peace due to her foul mouth, her habit of getting into dustups with her neighbors and her talent for eluding police.

Finding the constabulary at her door due to an alleged incident of vile language, she jumped out the back window of her apartment. She was apprehended and released on a fifty-dollar bail.

But when it came time to go to court to answer for her crimes, May was a no-show, and officers were sent by the court to haul her in. She led them on a wild chase through the waterfront lumberyards, where, in the towering rows, she eventually gave them the slip.

The elusive May Bee had been out of sight for a week when cops were called to deal with a commotion on Battery Street. The fracas involved half a dozen people, including May and two of her children. May, who police said could "lift her heels" and run like a deer, hightailed it out of there, but her son and daughter were arrested and received jail time—sixty and ninety days, respectively.

With May in hiding again, authorities planned and waited. One rainy day in October, after hearing news of her whereabouts, police closed in, but May was tipped off and bolted from the posse of patrolmen, fleeing in the rain down the Central Vermont Railroad tracks and into the Burlington Tunnel, she made her way to Winooski and temporary freedom.

On Tuesday, October 21, Monette, who had applied for a marriage license, went to Winooski to meet up with May. Little did he know that a Winooski police officer had been surveilling her as a favor to the Burlington Police. Instead of walking down the aisle, May was placed in custody.

Her would-be groom—apparently still very much in love—planned to ask for clemency in exchange for packing up May and her belongings once they were hitched and getting her the hell out of Burlington.

But authorities didn't just want Mrs. May Bee to go away, they wanted her far away. They gave her until midnight on October 30 to get out of Vermont; otherwise, she would serve a long term, eight months to three years, in the workhouse at the jail in Windsor. Presumably, she took the deal.

When she was last seen, May Bee had offended again, this time in New York, where authorities were able to catch up with her and bring her to justice with a term at the penitentiary in Albany.

7

THE MAN WHO STALKED HIS WIFE

I n 1926, Burlington had a front-row seat to a famously disastrous marriage: that of a local couple named Philip and Beatrice Heed, who entered into their state of matrimony in September 1925. By most accounts, Philip and "Bea," as her husband liked to call her, were a handsome couple, and at first, they were very much in love. But a little more than half a year after they said "I do," the bloom was off the rose.

Philip's wife, with her cloud of dark hair and sparkling eyes, was a popular gal with her choice of suitors before she fell for him. Imagine Philip's dismay when he learned that putting a ring on her finger didn't stop other fellows from admiring her.

The downside for Beatrice was discovering that Philip, who seemed such a catch when they first met, couldn't keep a job. And it wasn't just the fact he didn't work that bothered her, it was the reason: Philip left his shifts at the local woolen mills to stalk his wife in an effort to prevent her from being unfaithful.

As the old Cyndi Lauper song goes, "girls just want to have fun," but even when the Heeds had two incomes, Philip was not inclined to take his bride, a vivacious twenty-four-year-old, out on the town for the types of amusements that were popular in those days. With only one of them working, Beatrice was stuck at home without the small luxuries that might have distracted her. She grew just as tired of shouldering the burden of their household expenses as she was with Philip showing up at their home at 242 North Street in Burlington on the nights he was supposed to be working, thinking he'd catch her with another man.

They argued—and argued some more. Tensions grew as Beatrice began issuing ultimatums and threatening divorce.

By late February 1926, they were estranged, with Beatrice sleeping at her sister's home.

On the afternoon of March 2 at about 1:30 p.m., Beatrice stood at the jewelry counter just inside Green Brother's Five and Ten on Burlington's Church Street, laughing and gossiping while trying on rings. Normally, she worked the store's stocking counter, but because the place was fairly quiet that afternoon, she left her post to talk to her coworker Leona Lemieux.

While they chatted, the heavy entry door opened, letting in a gust of late winter air. Before Beatrice had a chance to turn, Philip entered the store, a .32-caliber Harrington and Richardson revolver in his hand. Without a moment's hesitation, he shot his wife three times in the back.

Leona Lemieux, who was standing next to Beatrice, screamed and fainted. She wasn't the only clerk to do so. Customers fled through the front doors onto Church Street as a frantic, bleeding Beatrice scrambled away from the counter, her husband not far behind.

Seeing Charles Murphy, the store's assistant manager, in the stairwell, Philip raised his hand over the head of a bewildered young male clerk, who ducked out of the way, aimed and fired. The shot was a miss. That was when Philip, to the shock of everyone watching, lifted the gun to his own head and pulled the trigger, slumping to the floor.

The couple lay close together, each in their own pool of blood. Philip, though wounded, managed to call out for a doctor, but Beatrice, her condition critical, still seemed to be the clearer headed of the two. When asked if she knew her name, she answered, "Yes. My name is Beatrice Heed." When an officer wanted to know if the man lying beside her was her husband, she said yes and then moaned, "Oh, I'm getting so weak, and I have such a pain in my heart!"

The couple was taken to the Mary Fletcher Hospital by ambulance. Police personnel reported that Philip said, loud enough for them to hear, "I'm sorry I did it, Beatrice. You know I love you."

Bleeding from three bullet wounds, Beatrice's situation was touch-and-go. As an officer carried her into the hospital and laid her gently on a bed, she looked into his eyes and asked, "Do you think I will get through this?" The cop knew things didn't look good.

The hospital's emergency staff set to work, knowing they were dealing with serious injuries. But of the two, Beatrice was the patient who caused them the gravest concern. This was a situation in which anything could

Burlington's Homeport store, the previous location of Green Brothers. *Roger Lewis.*

happen, despite their surgical expertise. Once they'd done everything they could, they held their collective breath.

Philip's condition was quick to improve, but Beatrice suffered complications. She spiked a fever, and doctors diagnosed her with pneumonia. Two of the bullets from her husband's gun had yet to be removed, but that would have to wait until—if ever—she gained back some of her strength.

Meanwhile, around town, the scandal was all anyone could talk about. People who knew the couple and even those who didn't couldn't stop speculating about what would make a man like Philip Heed attempt murder and then suicide so early in his marriage.

George Storti, the victim's brother-in-law, said Philip wasn't insane but went on record in the *Burlington Free Press* to say that Philip was "lazy and jealous of every man who looked at her."

Beatrice's coworkers were aware of the couple's marital issues. In the days before the shooting, one woman, Margaret Gravel, had prophetically asked Beatrice what she would do if Philip showed up at the store with a gun. "Why, he hasn't got the spunk to do that!" Beatrice replied, laughing.

By March 15, Philip was well enough to be released into police custody, but his court hearing was delayed while authorities waited for news about

Beatrice, who, they'd been told, was hovering between life and death, her mother keeping vigil at her bedside.

But Beatrice finally improved and began struggling through her long recovery. Seeing this, prosecutors wasted no time in making sure her husband paid for his crime.

On April 8 that year, Philip Heed, then just twenty-eight years old, pleaded guilty and was sentenced to serve twenty to twenty-five years in prison for assault with a deadly weapon and intent to kill. There was no reason for him to protest his innocence. He'd purchased the gun several days before the attempted murder and had been specific with the gun shop owner about the type of weapon he wanted. Also, tellingly, he had contacted the company that handled his and Beatrice's laundry the morning of the shooting to let them know their services would no longer be required. And of course, there were plenty of witnesses. He ended up serving less than half of his initial sentence at the Vermont State Prison in Windsor.

MRS. PHILIP HEED

Beatrice Heed. *From the* Burlington Daily News.

Beatrice filed for divorce in August that year, asking for permanent alimony, her lawyer stating she was no longer able to support herself due to the injuries she'd sustained by Philip's hand. Her divorce was granted the following November.

While Beatrice was indeed the victim of her husband's homicide attempt, during their marriage, she was probably not an innocent flower. Why? Because in August 1928, a few years into her husband's long prison term, Beatrice Heed, then known by her maiden name, Beatrice Lucia, was caught by authorities aiding a known smuggler, a barber who was about ten years her senior who also happened to be her married lover, during Prohibition. His name was Ernest Rubado.

A veteran of World War I, Ernest "Rube" Rubado's prior encounters with the authorities included charges of not only smuggling but also of gambling, drug use and disorderly conduct. He was already on probation after authorities caught him with a load of beer that included 408 bottles of Frontenac Special Canadian Ale.

During the August raid at Ernest's barbershop at 43 King Street, agents confiscated a quantity of home brew from the premises and reportedly would have seized more, except that upon their arrival, Beatrice, who had been staying with Rubado, evaded them and ran to the back of the establishment, where she began a frenzied smashing of bottles to get rid of the evidence. It was written in the local paper that she tussled vigorously with the investigators who entered the room to try to stop her.

At the ensuing trial, Rubado pleaded guilty and was sentenced to three to four months in the Vermont State Prison in Windsor. He was made to pay court fees of $17.60. Beatrice walked with no charges. But that wasn't the end of her troubles.

Five years later, on November 8, 1933, Beatrice was arrested and lodged in the Chittenden County Jail on charges of alienation of affections. The plaintiff? Mary Rubado, also known as *Mrs.* Ernest Rubado.

Mary, who had finally grown tired of her husband's illicit relationship, was suing Beatrice for $5,000 in cash. In her action, she claimed that several years earlier, she and her husband had been cohabitating quite happily when his "affection and regard" for her was destroyed by Miss Lucia, causing her to suffer "great distress of mind and body."

The suit was dropped from the docket, and the women settled out of court.

The following year, with Prohibition at an end, Beatrice Lucia Heed filed for and received a permit to sell beer out of an establishment on Burlington's Willow Street. Years later, on November 11, 1978, an obituary notice for Ernest "Rube" Rubado in the *Burlington Free Press* names his surviving wife as—if you can believe—Beatrice Lucia Rubado, whom he had married in March 1947.

Beatrice lived for five more years after Ernest's death. Her long and somewhat notorious life ended in October 1983. She was eighty-two. And that, as the late radio commentator Paul Harvey used to say, is the rest of the story.

8

THE UNINVITED WEDDING GUEST

I t used to be said that it was hard for a farmer to find a wife. Farm life can seem relentless and isolating. It's filled with daily tasks that can make or break your success. You're thwarted by weather. Income fluctuates. Those factors may have been on the mind of a young Vermont farmer named Maurice Poulin.

Poulin had found a girl, and she was lovely. She was twenty-four-year-old Eva LaCourse, a resident of Burlington. Eva, originally from St. Rosaire, Quebec, lived on Lakeside Avenue with her parents and worked, as many French Canadian residents of Burlington did, at the nearby Queen City Cotton Company. She was from a large family with her mother, father, three sisters and two brothers. Aside from her work at the mill, Eva had many friends and was active in her church, where she was a member of the Apostleship of Prayer, in which a person engaged in a morning prayer that devoted their day to God.

She and Poulin, who had been seeing each other for five years, had been engaged for a while. It's likely Eva started her relationship with Maurice, who was five years her senior, with the best intentions. But as she grew older, she may have realized just how much she would be missing if she left Burlington to spend most of her time in Essex, which, in those days, might have seemed almost a world away. She cared about Maurice, but she had reconsidered. She did not want to spend her life on a farm. She returned his ring.

Poulin, who had not been himself after the unexpected death of his father in September 1935, was devastated. He spent the days following the breakup not just bereft but almost in a state of panic, trying in vain to persuade Eva to change her mind, even warning her that he might do himself harm. Eva expressed concern about his rantings to a young woman she knew, who tossed the idea off. "That's just something you say. It's not something you do," the woman told her.

Poulin knew that on the morning of May 16, Eva was scheduled to attend a wedding and reception. He was invited to a wedding, too, the night before and begged her in a letter to accompany him. She declined, so he went to celebrate the evening wedding of his friend

Eva LaCourse in an undated photograph. *From the* Burlington Daily News.

Isidore Yandow alone. Eva was all he could talk about.

May 16, a Saturday, dawned bright and warm, the kind of spring day Vermonters look forward to all winter. Eva, dressed in her best outfit, headed to witness the nuptials of her friends Marie Adrienne Dore and Wilfred Mitchel Hamlin at St. Anthony's Church. The reception, or wedding breakfast, was held immediately afterward, hosted at the third-floor apartment of Mr. and Mrs. George Lebrun at 322 Flynn Avenue.

At around 9:00 a.m., Eva was called away by a friend. Maurice was there, uninvited; he said he needed to speak with her. Surprised and hoping to avoid a scene, Eva went down the stairs to the second-floor hall, where Poulin had entered the building. There, he begged her to take back her ring, to take *him* back. She declined. Starting up the stairs to make her way back to the party, she turned, telling him to go.

Wedding guests, hearing popping sounds, thought someone was playing with balloons, but it was no joke. Poulin had shot his former intended. A .38-caliber bullet passed through Eva's left breast and penetrated her lung, exiting below her left shoulder blade. A second shot entered above her hip, traveling through her stomach and intestines. Partygoers heard screams and ran into the hallway. Looking outside, they saw Poulin speed away in his car.

After shooting Eva, Maurice Poulin drove to the farm to bid farewell to his family. He told his mother he had shot his fiancée and then said, "And

St. Anthony's Church in Burlington's South End. *T. Lewis.*

now I'm going to drown myself." He set out to the Browns River covered bridge off route 128 in Westford, Vermont, with his younger siblings following at a distance. On the bridge, he shot himself in the chest and fell into the water. A neighbor, John Quinn, was fetched by Poulin's twelve-year-old sister, Florence. He fished Poulin out of the water and drove him to Fanny Allen Hospital.

At the Bishop DeGoesbriand Hospital in Burlington's Hill Section, Eva underwent multiple surgeries for her wounds and lay hovering between life and death. As pneumonia and sepsis set in, doctors knew there was little hope. She died three days after being shot by the man who professed to love her, but before she did, she described the crime to police. She gave the deathbed statement that State's Attorney K. Paul Fennell would use against Poulin in court.

Attorneys B.J. Leddy and Leon D. Latham lost no time in crafting a defense of temporary insanity. Poulin's brother, brother-in-law and even the deputy

Above: Brown's River Bridge. *Wikipedia.*

Opposite: Maurice Poulin. *From the* Burlington Daily News.

sheriff who guarded him said they believed he was not in his right mind. His brother Yvon told the court that while working on the farm, Poulin suffered hallucinations, frequently seeing a crowd of people who were watching him curiously. When Yvon visited his brother at Fanny Allen Hospital, Poulin wouldn't even talk to him. The sheriff said the young man would often call out for Eva and ask why she didn't visit him. Other witnesses said when they saw him in the hospital, he didn't seem to remember shooting himself and didn't even know how he'd gotten there.

Even his parish priest testified that his behavior before he shot Eva was abnormal. Poulin had gone to Father Pontbriand for advice, and the priest had assured him there were other fish in the sea. Poulin had cried out in despair, "No! Only one! Only one!"

More than one witness heard Poulin say he planned to drown himself, but no one suggested a doctor. The stigma around mental health issues was even stronger in those days than it is today.

As the trial wore on, Poulin sat quietly. It was difficult to tell what he was thinking as one female witness after another, friends of his dead fiancée, took

Maurice Poulin. *From the Burlington Daily News.*

the stand to talk about what had gone wrong with his ill-fated romance.

On January 18, 1937, Maurice Poulin, his eyes red from crying, was silent as he was brought to justice. He was found guilty by a jury of second-degree murder. He was given the maximum penalty for unpremeditated murder set down by the state: life of hard labor in the state's prison at Windsor.

In September 1944, eight years after murdering Eva LaCourse, Poulin took his own life, hanging himself from a rope tied to a beam in the prison boiler room.

9

BUDDY, CAN YOU SPARE A DIME?

In 1961, Burlington's downtown business district was plagued by a string of burglaries.

The targets were varied, and the culprits seemed, for a while, too slippery to catch.

Circumstances around the thefts began to make detectives in the Investigations Bureau of the Burlington Police Department (BPD) uneasy, since the hits at some of the locations would have been difficult or impossible for a thief to pull off without being seen by a patrolling officer.

Led by Detective Captain Arthur Carron, a probe that involved nearly five weeks of intensive undercover work and surveillance uncovered that the prime suspects were none other than Patrolmen John J. Malloy and John R. Adams. When the news broke in late December, it resulted in a crappy Christmas for all involved.

Adams and Malloy, who were each freed on $10,000 bail, pending trial, had very different reasons for committing the robberies. They stole from businesses that included the now-iconic Henry's Diner and Colonial Distributers, a location where the brazen Malloy actually went after a safe with a welding torch.

For Malloy, who'd read about a police burglary ring in Denver, Colorado, it was almost a lark. He wasn't sure why he started it. He claimed he didn't need the money, and what money he got was mostly frittered away, spent on things he couldn't even recall or treating his wife to a few extra bucks

John R. (Dick) Adams   **John J. Malloy**

BPD booking photographs of Officers Adams and Malloy. *Burlington Police.*

when she ran short on funds. Chatty with reporters who questioned him, Malloy said his criminal partnership with Adams, with whom he socialized regularly, was spur-of-the-moment. The two saw opportunities and took them. He claimed the pair hadn't made quite the haul they were accused of, saying he thought the amounts of the losses incurred by business owners was exaggerated.

Ironically, a break-in at the Above Par Restaurant on South Winooski Avenue, a job that allowed investigators nab the two, was the job Malloy had promised himself would be his last. He admitted that being caught made him feel small and that, overall, his comrades in the department were good, honest officers. But, he said, "I don't think anyone realizes the very great temptation a policeman faces—and the small amount of money he is paid."

Burlington citizens would eventually get a glimpse of exactly what Malloy was talking about. Irrespective of the officers' breach of trust, there was a big problem in the department: low pay.

While reluctant to get into the nitty gritty of his financial situation, Officer Adams, a war veteran who was later described in court as coming from "an excellent family," said he lived the double life of criminal and public servant simply because he needed the money. He was, he said, "up to his ears" in debt, telling a reporter who questioned him, "You can put down that the low pay that policemen get had something to do with this."

Looking at the median income for families living in the United States in 1961, he wasn't wrong. The pretax income of the average American family that year was about $5,700. Adams's pretax income was $4,107, over $1,500 *less* than the average. And his pay was typical of other members of the force who had served between three and five years. Of the forty-nine officers employed by the Burlington Police Department at that time, over half were holding down part-time jobs in addition to their work on the force.

Malloy and Adams, who admitted to burglarizing ten businesses in all, cooperated fully with investigators. Pleading guilty, they were each sentenced to four to six years in the state prison at Windsor.

But there was more bad news to come. On January 12, 1962, three more officers were charged.

Burlington Police Department, late 1950s. *University of Vermont Libraries, Special Collections.*

Officers William J. Bleau Jr., Richard D. Bates and Harry J. Muir were pinned with victimizing the merchants they'd sworn to protect at businesses that included the S.R. Saiger Company on Pine Street and Magrams Fashion Shop, a popular department store on Church Street. All three pleaded not guilty, and each were released on $3,500 bail. They resigned, as did Adams and Malloy before them. During the investigation of the crimes committed by the officers, it was discovered that not all the merchandise that had been stolen were big-ticket items or luxuries; instead, they included things like baby food and false teeth powder. Captain George A. McKenzie, who would become interim chief during the dishonorable episode, called the three men "financially destitute."

After a period of maintaining their innocence, Bleu and Bates reversed their pleas and were tried in March 1962. Bates, the older of the two, was sentenced to eighteen to thirty-six months in prison. Bleau, who had admitted to stealing coffee, ketchup, a maternity dress, a bassinet and other sundry items, got a lighter sentence of eight to twenty-four months in prison.

Muir, however, continued to maintain his innocence. His lawyer, John B. Harrington, believing it would be hard to find impartial jurors close to home, asked for a change of venue, his preference being Bennington. It was eventually decided that Muir's trial would be held in faraway Windsor County. But on October 5, with his trial imminent, Muir, a married father of two, reversed his plea. The young patrolman, who had stolen from Magrams, was handed a lighter sentence than the others, six to twenty-four months in prison, with all but the first six suspended. Judge Rudolph J. Daley considered Muir's age and time on the force and the fact he had no previous record. Also a factor was that the value of the goods he took was less than $100. As the judge handed down his sentence, Muir's young wife burst into tears.

In addition to the five officers who were charged with theft, two officers, William G. Croll and Robert J. Martin, were suspended without pay for two weeks for "violation of department regulations."

The crime spree perpetrated by members of the Queen City's police department was big news outside of Burlington. *Life* magazine ran a huge spread on the case, adding to the department's woes. Public sentiment against BPD was at an all-time low, as it seemed the entire force was painted with the brush of scandal.

Ultimately, the investigation was expanded, delving into the backgrounds and actions of each officer on the force, whether they were suspected of criminal activity or not. One-term mayor Robert K. Bing, who, years later,

Burlington Police Department, 1960s. *University of Vermont Libraries, Special Collections.*

would be named the executive director of Vermont governor Deane Davis' Commission on Crime Control and Prevention, called for an inquisition of the officers who remained, including then-acting chief McKenzie and Detective Captain Carron, the men who had arrested the rogue officers. One by one, employees of the department were called to swear an oath and submit to questioning about their conduct while on the force. Some, who'd had nothing to do with the burglaries, resigned. Others, out on the street, had to shoulder the stigma in the aftermath of the felonious acts committed by those who'd been charged.

It was a topsy-turvy time. Specialists from the International Police Chiefs Association in Washington, D.C., were called to Burlington to diagnose the issues in the department, a survey that would cost the city $4,000, the equivalent of about $40,246 today. The goal was to "effect policy changes that will transform the force into a streamlined, skillful law-enforcement agency."

Acting chief McKenzie, who'd instigated the police survey and who was found not guilty of any wrongdoing during Bing's inquisition, resigned. The career cop, who had once talked a man with a ten-inch knife out of jumping into the Winooski River, was expected to be appointed to the position for the long term. Instead, he took on work as a special investigator with local attorneys and insurance companies.

With McKenzie's resignation, Detective Captain Carron was named acting chief. He would remain Burlington's chief of police until 1974.

10

DON'T BLAME IT ON BUNDY

It's not often that a cold case gets solved *while* I'm writing about it, but that's what happened while I was writing about the more than fifty-year-old murder investigation of Rita Curran, a beloved second grade teacher from Milton, Vermont. In the end, all it took was some DNA evidence and a confession from the woman who had given the murderer his alibi.

Rita Curran was born on June 21, 1947, in Brooklyn, New York. By all accounts a sweet, quiet young woman, she lived at home with her parents until the summer of 1971. She was a public school teacher who also taught religion classes at St. Anne's Church in Milton.

After seeing an advertisement in a local paper for a short-term roommate, Rita moved into an apartment at 17 Brookes Avenue, close to the University of Vermont's campus and convenient for the reading and language arts classes she was taking as part of a graduate program. Rita was also employed at the Colonial Motor Inn on Shelburne Road, a job she'd held every summer for four years, having started there when she was still a student at Trinity College. Popular with the rest of the staff at the inn, she often joked to them that she was "an ugly duckling," revealing that the summer she'd moved to Burlington she'd already attended three weddings (she'd been an attendant in at least two) and had to leave Milton because all the eligible young men there were taken.

Rita's chambermaid shifts at the motel ended around midafternoon, giving her time for recreational pursuits.

Milton teacher Rita Curran. *WCAX-TV.*

She'd recently joined a barbershop quartet that met at a local community center in Burlington's Old North End, and she was with them on the evening of Monday, July 19.

She returned home from rehearsals at the Sarah Holbrook Center at about ten. Her roommate Beverly Lamphere said she last spoke with Rita before she left the house at 11:20 p.m. to meet their third roommate, Kerry Duane, and her good friend Paul Robinson for a late bite at a restaurant on Shelburne Road. Rita, who declined an invitation to join them, had been in their shared room, already preparing for bed.

When the three returned to the apartment, they spent over an hour laughing and talking in the living room, totally unaware of the scene that awaited them just beyond Rita's closed bedroom door.

When Lamphere finally entered her bedroom, she was shocked by what she found: her petite roommate lying on her back, motionless, just inside the bedroom door. Rita was nude, her face spattered with blood. A torn pair of underpants was partially hidden by her too-still body.

The police were alerted, and when they arrived, they began trying to make sense of the scene. None of the windows in the apartment had been tampered with. The killer had to have entered through the front or back door, neither of which had been locked. Rita's purse, undisturbed, was behind the bedroom door, with all her cash, her driver's license and personal papers still inside. Police found blood on the floor in the kitchen by the back door, an indication that whoever had committed the crime had exited that way. Detectives closed off the area and worked through the night to gather every bit of evidence they could. Rita Curran had died from asphyxiation and multiple blows to the face and head. She had been sexually assaulted. The race was on to find her killer.

The police examined Rita's car. It was parked in front of the apartment, and there was no indication anyone else had been inside it. They questioned neighbors. They all said they hadn't heard a thing, not a struggle or a scream in the night, which is astounding, since medical examiner Dr. Lawrence Harris said there were signs of "an intense struggle." Rita Curran had fought hard for her life.

There was an initial press release about the murder, and while police gathered more forensic evidence, a stunned community buzzed with the

Rita Curran's Brookes Avenue home. *T. Lewis.*

news, worried that they might also be in danger. Over the next several days, all over the small city in which people rarely locked their doors, hardware stores were selling out of bolt locks. A woman at one store bought seven window locks. Police Chief Arthur Carron recommended outside lights be left on at night. While authorities grappled with solving the crime, pranksters preyed on the fears of the town's vulnerable young women with hang-up calls. There were also reports to local police of "peeping Toms."

Authorities were in a fix. There was, understandably, a lot of pressure on them to find the young teacher's killer. But there were no immediate leads.

Former Vermont senator Patrick Leahy, Chittenden County's state's attorney at the time, was, by necessity, shuffling other business to the side. When a training exercise, the burning of a local country club, caused someone to file a complaint of air pollution, he told the *Burlington Free Press*, "I'm not going to have a chance to look into anything else at this time. The Rita Curran murder is taking top priority in this office."

There were three detectives working on the case. One, Lieutenant Beaulieu, had visited with Rita's family in Milton to obtain more biographical information about her and learn about her friends. More than one hundred people had been questioned. At least three people who knew her submitted to lie detector tests.

On Friday, July 23, the day of Rita's funeral, a crowd that numbered over three hundred gathered to pay their respects, most of them unaware that plainclothes policemen sat among them.

The Wednesday before the funeral, authorities started a roundup of the area's known sex offenders.

Citing new and "encouraging" leads, Leahy said the rest of the investigation would be conducted in secrecy. A blackout was issued on the release of information about the case, with any details needing to be cleared by him or Beaulieu.

It was revealed Burlington Police identification officer Harold Baker was to fly to Washington to meet with the FBI experts who were analyzing evidence gathered by the BPD. They were doing this to eliminate the lag time normally associated with getting information from the federal department. The move was instigated at the suggestion of Pat Leahy, who believed every hour was critical.

By July 28, there was still nothing new to report about the case. The apartment Rita had shared, previously sealed off to anyone but investigators since her murder, had been released back to its owner Timothee Tessier. Her roommates were free to return, though it was Lieutenant Beaulieu's belief that they were finding other accommodations.

By August, the murder still hadn't been solved, and police and Pat Leahy were leaving no stone unturned. There was an Associated Press report that said a Charles Manning of Providence, Rhode Island, had been investigated on a burglary charge and was undergoing a psychiatric evaluation at Bridgewater State Hospital. Manning claimed to have killed nineteen women, including Valerie Percy, the daughter of Senator Charles Percy of Illinois in September 1966. It was not known whether Manning had ever been in the Burlington area, but it was worth checking out.

On August 28, a woman on Greene Street in Burlington suffered an attempted sexual assault. Her assailant was a twenty-eight-year-old unemployed man named Bruce Alicandry. Neighbors heard the woman's screams and called the police. It was the first assault of its kind since the crime on Brookes Avenue, and the locations of these crimes were not even a half mile apart. Police were closed-mouthed about whether the incident could be related.

On September 1, a joint news conference was held by Leahy and Beaulieu. The news blackout was lifted. The police had discovered there was no connection between the assault on Greene Street and the Curran murder. There were no new leads. No arrests were imminent.

Citing an issue with staffing, Beaulieu conceded his team was no longer surveilling the Brookes Avenue area. Leahy added that the team had already spent upward of one thousand man hours on the investigation and had tracked down hundreds of leads.

A young Senator Patrick Leahy. *U.S. Senate Archives.*

One thing the press conference did reveal was that after Rita's murder, many young women came forward to offer information. They admitted to being sexually assaulted but said they had been too afraid to report, not surprising since a female victim of rape in the 1970s was likely to be treated like a criminal or, at the very least, like she'd been "asking for it."

The investigation into Rita's murder continued, with all but one investigator, Sergeant Wayne Liberty, dropping from the case by mid-September. Disappointingly, evidence submitted to the FBI that authorities once found encouraging did not pan out.

In October 1971, the *Burlington Free Press* reported that a UVM coed was attacked in her apartment. The twenty-one-year-old woke to find a man on top of her. When she screamed, he struck her several times in the head. Her two housemates heard the noise, and when they came to her aid, the assailant fled. She could give no description of the assailant due to the darkness of her room. The South Union Street attack was the fifth such incident to occur in the city in a month, with most of the attacks or break-ins occurring mere blocks from Rita's old apartment.

The city's mayor Gordon Paquette was being urged to fortify the police department, with one city alderman suggesting an emergency loan to cover officer salaries. Paquette cautioned that more police officers were not necessarily the answer to Burlington's crime problem. He asked, "What are we going to do, have police on every street?...What we have here is a real problem. And it's going to be real tough to solve." He noted that Burlington residents had to do their share to solve the crime problem through increased participation. He also realized there might be some psychological shock for people who'd never before had to worry about avoiding dark streets or walking alone as they modified their behavior: "But they have to do so until such time as we curb this crime and catch the criminals that are causing so much fear in this city."

In December, with Rita's murder unsolved but not forgotten, a reward was offered in the pages of the *Burlington Free Press*, funded by the paper itself. Called a "Secret Witness Reward," it offered $3,000 for information leading to the conviction of the killer. The program gave explicit instructions for how letters should be formatted and dedicated one individual at the *Burlington Free Press* who would serve as a contact. It also assured absolute anonymity. The information had to be certified and had to lead to the arrest and conviction of the perpetrator. Letters providing information remained anonymous through the implementation of special code numbers. The reward would be paid through a third party.

The Rita Curran Murder wasn't the only crime the paper was trying to solve. It was also looking for an arsonist who'd set the fire that destroyed Burlington's Strong Theater building and whoever had incinerated a couple of vehicles, including (the dream car of my youth) a Plymouth Barracuda.

By April 1972, Rita's killer still hadn't been found. Authorities assured the public that whenever they heard of a similar crime anywhere in New England or New York, they immediately contacted the investigating department. The *Burlington Free Press*'s reward was offered through March 1973, but no viable leads were provided.

In 1981, nearly ten years after Rita's murder, Angela Belisle, a mother of three, was killed outside her home on Brookes Avenue, bringing Rita's case back into the news. In a strange twist, Belisle had also been an elementary school teacher, but the cases were otherwise unrelated.

In 1989, Rita's unsolved murder case took an interesting turn. There was a new suspect, one whose name had recently been on the lips of people all over the country: Ted Bundy.

Bundy, arguably one of the most well-known serial killers of the twentieth century, was born in Burlington at a haven for unwed mothers, the Lund Home, previously named the Home for Friendless Women.

While he didn't grow up in Burlington, it was speculated, largely due to information provided by renowned true crime author Anne Rule in her blockbuster book *The Stranger Beside Me*, that Bundy had come back to Burlington to check out the origins of his birth. It seemed entirely plausible that Bundy, a charming sociopath who, between 1974 and 1978, raped and murdered more than twenty-five girls and women, might be Rita's killer as well. Known for his attraction to long-haired brunettes, his typical modus operandi was to strangle and bludgeon his victims. Rita had been beaten about the face and strangled.

Ted Bundy in custody. *Florida Department of Corrections.*

In the hubbub after Bundy's execution on January 24, 1989, Rita's sister Mary Campbell told reporters she believed Bundy might be her sister's killer. She had even written Bundy a letter, asking if he had murdered her Rita. The FBI sent back information revealing that during interrogation, Bundy did not confirm nor deny committing the crime. Years passed with nothing but more speculation.

In 2016, while working on stories for my true crime bus tour, I filed an information request with the Burlington Police Department for Rita's case, a request they denied citing the ongoing investigation.

Responses I got whenever I talked about the case were a mixed bag. I was chastised by a few people who felt the topic was taboo and that I was being insensitive to the feelings of her remaining family. A family member came to my defense in a Facebook forum, saying the only way her killer would ever be found was if people kept her story in the public view. More than ever, I wanted to see her killer found.

Rita Curran's murderer, William DeRoos. *WCAX-TV.*

Then, on February 16, 2023, startling news came: the Burlington Police Department was going to conduct a press conference the following Tuesday to reveal they'd solved the Curran murder. On that day, we finally learned Rita Curran had been killed by a man named William DeRoos, who lived in an apartment two floors above hers. Though he had an alibi, he'd remained a suspect.

DeRoos, who'd been married only a few weeks at the time of Rita's murder, had an argument with his wife that evening and left the apartment for a cooling-off period. He then entered Rita's apartment, killing her during the seventy-minute window in which her roommates were absent. When detectives first questioned DeRoos and his wife, Michelle, the following morning, the couple said they'd both been home and hadn't seen or heard anything. But there was a piece of evidence left at the scene that gave lie to that claim: a cigarette butt next to Curran's body. When the cigarette was tested over five decades later, it was found to contain DNA that matched that of DeRoos's half-brother.

When police reinterviewed DeRoos's ex-wife, she admitted her husband *had* left their apartment during the time Curran's roommates were having their late meal. Burlington Police lieutenant James Trieb said, "Immediately upon closing the door [after police questioning]…he [DeRoos] turned to Michelle and told her that if the police ever showed up again, she was to tell them that he was home all night." Burlington Police detective Corporal Thomas Chenette commented at the press conference, "I think she lied at the time because she was young. She was naive. She was newly married. She was in love."

Michelle, who now lives on the West Coast, revealed to authorities she'd been afraid of her husband, who had an explosive temper. She described that one night, when the two were having dinner, for no reason (at least none that she could discern), DeRoos jumped up and strangled her with both of his hands. After the two divorced, he left the country to become a Buddhist monk, eventually returning to the United States and life in San Francisco with a new wife, who also suffered his abuse. Once, DeRoos choked her until she was unconscious, and on another occasion, he stabbed one of her friends for no reason.

DeRoos died in 1986 of a drug overdose at the age of forty-six. The case that Corporal Tom Chenette of the Burlington Police called "the most investigated case the Burlington Police Department ever had" is now closed. Rita's parents never got to see the case solved, but there's finally closure for her sister, Mary, and brother, Tom, and the rest of the Curran family.

11

MURDER AT THE SYNAGOGUE

F *ilicide*: the term for a parent killing a child. It's an act found throughout history in literature and in life. It happened in Burlington on May 6, 1977, when a woman named Marilyn Dietl premeditatedly took her daughter's life in the parking lot of a popular local thrift store. Judy Dietl, not quite twenty years old, didn't deserve to die, but her mother thought she should, believing it would save her from a fate worse than death.

Judy was born to Marilyn and her husband, Frank, on July 8, 1959. Growing up in Malletts Bay in Colchester, Vermont, with her brother, Robert, and three sisters, Deborah Ann, Dawn Marie and Kim Francine, she lived a comfortable, middle-class life.

Judy's high school principal, Robert Burke, described her as a nice kid who never got into trouble. Voted one of the prettiest girls in her class, she didn't participate in school activities, had no boyfriends and didn't attend prom. Away from school, she could most likely be found working at her parent's Carvelle ice cream shop in Burlington's North Avenue Shopping Plaza.

After she graduated from Colchester High School in 1977, the girl who was described as always being "good" moved to Boston to attend college, spurring a new friction between her and her parents.

Judy wanted to be an airline hostess, so she picked a school with a program that would give her the necessary experience. She and her friend Diane Brochu, who was also attending college in the Boston area, rented a room at the YWCA on Boston's Berkeley Street.

Judy Dietl in an undated yearbook photograph. *From the* Colchester High School Venture.

The girls would often stop at a neighborhood store to buy snacks to bring back to their room. At the store, they met two men, Louis and Damon, employees there. Both men were Black. Eventually, Louis and Damon asked them out. In a letter to her sister Deborah, Judy wrote, "Two guys took us out. We had a great time.... They must have spent at least a $100 on us." Later, she wrote, "It's like a dream and I don't want to wake up. This is not like Vermont at all."

Knowing their mother wouldn't approve, Judy asked her sister to remain quiet about the news, and Deborah did—for a while. Eventually, though, she called her father and told him Judy was seeing a guy who was buying her presents.

He seemed unfazed, saying if this guy wanted to spend money on Judy, let him spend it—that is, until his daughter said, "But, he's Black...and I think he's a pimp."

Frank, Marilyn and Diane's mother, Virginia Brochu, hopped on a bus to Boston with the intention of getting to the bottom of the situation and straightening the girls out. When Judy protested that the men just wanted to date them, Marilyn found a darker motive, saying the men, who were buying the two young girls drinks and giving them gifts, were grooming them for something sinister. Judy promised to stop seeing Damon.

Back in Vermont, Judy's parents were on edge. Their girl had always done as she was told. As Marilyn would later sob in court while recalling Judy before Boston, "She didn't give me any problems at all." Her parents said they feared she was a girl who could be swayed. Her father said, "She didn't really have a mind of her own."

When Christmas break came, Judy wanted to spend her time in Boston. Instead, her parents sent her off to visit her grandmother. During that time, Marilyn confronted her, saying she thought she was still seeing Damon. Judy was but told her mother she wasn't.

A few months later, in February, Judy called her family to tell them about a massive snowstorm that had hit Boston and to give them news about her grades. What she didn't tell them was Diane was no longer with her and that she'd quit school, something Marilyn learned from a distraught Virginia. During a phone conversation with Judy, Marilyn found out her daughter planned to stay in Boston.

According to Marilyn, Diane confessed "everything" to her mother. The girls were still seeing Louis and Damon, but Diane felt she was "in too deep" and decided to leave. Virginia told Marilyn that Diane had told her Judy "wasn't afraid of her father" anymore.

Not waiting to consult with Frank, who was away on business, Marilyn went alone to Boston, where she surprised Judy in her room. She accused her of lying and began searching the place for clues. She claimed she found a laminated ID card with Judy's picture but someone else's name. She said she also found notes and gifts from Damon and that while checking Judy's bank book, she found two large withdrawals, loans to Damon. She surmised that Damon was bleeding Judy of cash to make her dependent on him in order to lure her into a life of prostitution. She told her daughter to pack her belongings. She was taking her home.

Judy did go back to Vermont. But two days later, she left the house with the intention to go back to Boston. Marilyn, alerted by Judy's siblings, found her at the bus terminal and ordered her into the car, where she grabbed her by the hair. She later claimed the girl left home because she didn't want to face her father. Frank returned that night, but he and his daughter didn't speak, as Judy was already asleep.

Accounts say sometime later, Judy would write Diane, who was back in Boston, saying she was afraid to talk with Frank because she didn't want to "get beat up." Based on media reports, there seemed to be a lot of concern in the Dietl household when it came to not upsetting "Daddy."

Judy told Diane she missed her and Damon and Louis. In Vermont, she was under guard, accompanied everywhere she went. At some point, Damon began calling the Dietl house. Marilyn claimed she heard a conversation in which Damon and Judy argued over her not returning to Boston, and she had thought, "I'm winning." She was hoping Damon would be mad at Judy and stop calling. But shortly afterward, Judy told her she was going back to Boston.

Marilyn said she pleaded with her husband to help her change Judy's mind, and according to newspaper accounts of their conversation, he said he would. But because their other children were nearby, he didn't. Marilyn claimed that by that time, Judy had admitted "she knew Damon was a pimp." Oddly, Marilyn said she didn't pass that information along to Frank.

This alleged fact about Damon, along with Judy's desire to return to Boston, was preying on Marilyn's mind. On the night of May 5, she was unable to sleep and woke up exhausted. After getting the younger kids off to school, she lay down to take a nap. She told the court she woke up to a "message" in her head: "This is the day she dies."

As she went about her usual household chores, Marilyn got her husband's old .38-caliber revolver, left over from his days as an auxiliary policeman, from a shelf in a bedroom closet. She loaded it and tucked it into her purse. When the kids returned from school, she went to Judy's room and told her to come with her. Before she left the house with her daughter one last time, the gun tucked away in her bag, she issued instructions to young Dawn Marie to be sure to start the rice for their dinner at 5:30 p.m. Then she got into the car and drove with Judy to the parking lot of the Shalom Shuk thrift store behind the Ohavi Sedek Synagogue on North Prospect Street in Burlington. They'd often gone there together to shop for secondhand clothing. It was a place, she admitted later, that she chose because it was out of the public view.

Judy got out of the car, her mother behind her. Marilyn told her to try the thrift store door. Judy did and then turned around to say it was locked. She saw her mother with the gun and cried, "No! No! No!" Marilyn Dietl fired over and over again, six times in all, saying, "Judy, I can't let you go."

Afterward, Marilyn went to a nearby home and asked the resident to call the police. She then went back to the parking lot, took a blanket from the back of the car and covered her daughter with it. She noticed an ant crawling on her daughter's face and brushed it off. She told Judy she was sorry but later admitted that in that moment, she wasn't. She would do anything to protect her child—even if it meant killing her.

Judy died from her wounds several hours later.

Ohavi Sedek Synagogue. *Roger Lewis.*

Shalom Shuk Thrift Store. *Roger Lewis.*

Marilyn Dietl entered a plea of not guilty. Her bail was set at $25,000. Experts who were called in to evaluate her state of mind when she killed Judy said that while she was sane at the time she pulled the trigger, she was in a "dissociated" state of mind.

Marilyn maintained she *had* to shoot Judy to save her from life of prostitution. When asked, "Was it your intention to kill your daughter when you took the gun from the closet?" Dietl said Judy was already dead that day because of the message she'd gotten the morning of the murder. "When it happened," she said, "I felt such a relief that she was safe."

Marilyn Dietl was said to be a religious, morally upright person. Her husband, Frank, shed some light on her act when he said that Marilyn's family had discovered one of her grandmothers was "a girl from the islands," a prostitute in the Dutch East Indies, and his wife told him her family had taunted her that if anyone in the family was going to go bad, it was her. She was always on guard for the appearance of impropriety. Frank said when he was in the navy and Marilyn was just a girl of sixteen, she would make herself so nervous before their dates that she would become ill.

There's no proof Judy Dietl wanted to go back to Boston so she could live a life of prostitution. In speaking with Mark Keller, who was Chittenden County's state's attorney at the time, it became clear that Dietl, no longer able to control Judy and fearing social stigma due to her own family baggage, simply snapped. As Keller put it, she was "delusional."

The papers didn't play it that way. Rather than focus on how Marilyn could have cold-bloodedly killed her child, they seemed to take her account as gospel. It was the late '70s, and it was easier to lay the blame on an elusive, "Black pimp" than to examine a mental health issue that resulted in the death of a girl with her entire life ahead of her.

There was a lot of public sympathy for Marilyn. Many in the community, swayed by her story, felt the forty-year-old mother had been through enough and should be spared jail time. After all, she still had family left who needed her. But Judge Gibson, weighing the situation, thought otherwise, saying, "It's not up to another person, even a mother, to make [a] life decision for that person."

In November 1978, Marilyn Dietl, her charge reduced, was sentenced to five to fifteen years in prison for second-degree murder.

In June 1980, the *Rutland Herald* revealed that Marilyn, considered a model prisoner (Keller told me she was called "Mom" by the other inmates), had been allowed to leave the Chittenden Community Correctional Center on work furlough a year after her sentencing. Where was she working? At the family ice cream parlor.

12

A VERY COLD CASE

Two schoolteachers were murdered ten years apart on the same quiet street. Mind boggling, right? An even more startling fact is that both of the murders went unsolved for more than fifty years.

The first case, that of Rita Curran, mentioned earlier in this book, was solved in 2023. But the killer of Angela Belisle, who was murdered on a frigid January night in 1981, remains elusive.

Around 10:45 a.m. on January 3, 1981, the frozen body of Angela Belisle was found lying beside her car, parked in front of 62 Brooks Avenue, by Mark Hassinger, a student at nearby UVM. At first glance, he thought what he saw was a mannequin. (Hearing this bit of information, a guest on my true crime bus tour remarked, "It's never a mannequin.") But after peering down at her, he realized this was no dummy and ran to the nearby home of Vince Grove to call the police. Afterward, the two went back to the car together to get a closer look. There was snow on the ground but none on the victim. They noticed her body was bloody, her skin beige.

When police arrived on the scene, they initially thought Belisle, who was lying on her back near the driver's side of the vehicle, had slipped and died of exposure. Burlington officer Patrick Foley stated, "It appeared as if she stepped out of her vehicle, lost her balance, fell, banged her head, and pretty much froze to death." There were no apparent signs of a struggle or footprints in the snow around her body. Upon closer examination, however, he discovered she'd been shot in the front of the head, apparently at close range. State's Attorney Mark Keller was called.

The 62 Brookes Avenue home of Angela Belisle. *T. Lewis.*

Belisle had actually been shot twice, but there were no witnesses and neighbors couldn't even recall hearing gunshots. Police, while searching the area for evidence, never found a weapon. They did find a bullet on the ground while methodically scooping up and melting the snow. Forensics could tell them more, but they would have to wait. Chief Medical Examiner Eleanor McQuillan said it wasn't unusual for a body to take a few days to thaw enough for an examination. When she was able to examine Belisle's body, she couldn't pinpoint an exact time of death due to the frigid temperatures the night the woman was killed.

Robbery wasn't a motive—Belisle had her purse with her, and the contents were undisturbed. A search of her car revealed she'd bought groceries before she was murdered. With her children off with their father, she was probably looking forward to an uneventful evening.

Time went by with no arrests. As the police continued to interview persons of interest, the word was they weren't ruling out a murder-for-hire scenario. But who would want Angela Belisle dead?

Angela Belisle was born Angela Louise Gage on December 5, 1945. She attended college for two years and obtained her teaching certificate before meeting Gerald "Jerry" Belisle, a cement truck driver for the S.T. Griswold Company, at a dance in Bedford, Quebec. They were married in 1968.

The couple settled in Swanton, Vermont, and went on to have three children together: Selena in December 1970, Travis in April 1972 and Trevor in February 1974.

Angela got a job teaching first grade in nearby St. Albans as Jerry built his cement pouring company. Financially, the couple was thriving; they built a new home and bought a camp on Lake Champlain.

By that time, however, they were often at odds. They decided to get a divorce, which was finalized in 1979. But after the camp that Angela was awarded in the dissolution of her marriage was vandalized and her home destroyed by fire, she began to be concerned for her personal safety. In 1980, she and her kids moved to Burlington.

Angela, who was described by one of her neighbors as "a professional woman," was attending UVM and working toward a graduate degree in psychology. She was well liked by her neighbors, who remarked her children were "beautiful," well-cared-for and well-behaved.

The December before her murder, Angela petitioned the Franklin County Superior Court to reopen her divorce case. She wanted the summer camp's appraisal adjusted and a modification made to her child support payments. A hearing was set for January 14, 1981, a few weeks after her murder.

You might wonder, in light of this bit of information, whether Jerry Belisle felt a certain way about her request and decided to do something about it, but Jerry Belisle had an alibi. He'd picked up the kids from his ex-wife at a UVM parking lot at 6:00 p.m. the night of the murder. He told authorities he'd taken them to his home in St. Albans. When questioned about the evening, his daughter Selena, who was ten at the time, told police she woke up in the middle of the night to find her father snoring on the living room floor. She said she remembered the time, 12:34 a.m. because she had looked at the digital clock. When asked about years later in a retrospective article about the case, she said she remembered because, "It's rare to see it [the clock] with the numbers 1, 2, 3, 4 in a row like that."

On January 5, 1981, an inquest was held. (Inquests are held when witnesses refuse to cooperate with investigators and are called in to answer questions under oath.) Keller refused to say who had been subpoenaed, but he did say the effort had been "disappointing." He mentioned they might be bringing the subject in again later in the week.

Angela and Jerry Belisle in happier times. *From the Stanstead Journal.*

Angela's body was taken home to Quebec for her funeral. Around that time, a friend she'd confided in who did not want to be named said Angela, in the time before her murder, had become fearful for her life. The friend said she seldom went out at night, and when she did, she made sure to park her car in such a way that she had the shortest walk possible to her front door. When told this by a reporter, Jerry Belisle said he knew his ex-wife was afraid but didn't know why; he declined further comment.

There were more inquests. Polygraph tests were given to a few potential witnesses, but there were still no breaks in the case. Ballistics examined bullet fragments to determine what kind of gun was used, but that was of little help, since there was still no murder weapon.

In March 1981, with the investigation ongoing, David Harrison of Highgate, Jerry Belisle's longtime business partner in the company Harrison-Belisle Co. Inc., was found dead by suicide. He left no note. It was acknowledged that he had been questioned at an inquest in connection with Angela Belisle's murder, but he wasn't considered a suspect.

Looking at the case, I was surprised to note the Belisles seemed plagued by fires. There was the one that destroyed Angela's home after her separation from Jerry and another in October 1994 that struck a property Jerry owned that housed a business called Bakersfield Hardware. Investigators said that fire was the result of a break-in and had been intentionally set. In January 1997, Angela's old camp at Lapans Bay on Lake Champlain burned to the ground. It was for sale at the time. Then, in July 1997, a fire on lower Newton Street in St. Albans destroyed a carpet store, a tanning salon, a real estate office, a sign company and Jerry Belisle's business City Feed and Lumber Company. According to the *Burlington Free Press*, Jerry owned the lion's share of the business complex. Losses were in the millions.

I'm inclined to believe we'll never know who killed Angela Belisle, but with the Rita Curran case being solved after more than fifty years, I've learned to never say never.

The Vermont State Police are still accepting information. Their Major Crime Unit can be reached by calling 802-244-8781 or by writing vtips.info. Anyone with information will remain anonymous.

13

STATE V. HAMLIN

In the 1980s, Burlington's Old North End neighborhood was a place where it was hard to be anonymous. Not only did everyone seem to know everyone, but they also knew their business. The gossip mill in the tightly knit community could be counted on to run in high gear. Sometimes, the most jaw-dropping and scandalous stories started with the slimmest tidbit of information, something that seemed innocent until it wasn't.

That's how it was the day my younger brother, Will, came home from Burlington High School and began rummaging through the fridge while giving me a blow by blow of his day. He mentioned that a classmate of his, Louis "Louie" Hamlin, had shaved his beard.

Hamlin's beard would have been impressive on a man twice his age and had always seemed incongruous to me on a teenager. I tried for a second to imagine the sixteen-year-old without it but couldn't. "Man," I remarked. "He must look completely different."

"Yup," Will chuckled through bites of cold pizza. "Now he looks twenty instead of thirty."

It was a while before we connected Hamlin to what was playing out in the news: the police were searching for two men who had killed a middle-schooler in the town of Essex Junction the Friday before. I guess we were too naïive to wrap our heads around a high school student, a sixteen-year-old we knew, being capable of such a thing.

Today, over forty years later, it's hard to find a Vermonter who was alive on Friday, May 15, 1981, who doesn't know the story of how a Central

Vermont Railroad dispatcher, Alton Bruso, was going about his work, watching a slow-moving train make its rounds near Maple Street Park at about 4:40 p.m., when he noticed a little girl coming toward him along the tracks. From a distance, she appeared to be wearing a red bathing suit, but as she got closer, Bruso realized she wasn't wearing clothing at all—most of her nude body was covered in blood. Bruso ran toward her, all the while shouting into his walkie-talkie for someone to stop the train. Closing the gap between them, Bruso heard the girl say, before she collapsed, "Please help me, sir. I've been raped." Watching air bubbles emerge from a wound in her chest, Bruso shouted into his radio for someone to call the police and rescue workers. He held the girl, his hand over a stream of blood, trying to staunch its flow, and waited.

The injured girl was twelve-year-old Megan O'Rourke. She and her friend Melissa Walbridge, thirteen, had been walking home from Albert D. Laughton Middle School when they took a popular shortcut through Maple Street Park, past the tennis courts and into a wooded area that would bring them to the section of town where the streets were named after Native tribes, a place known to the locals as Indian Acres. It was a walk they'd taken together countless times without incident that, on this particular day, ended in tragedy.

Maple Street Park. *Roger Lewis.*

Megan was carried by railroad workers to where first responders, shocked by what they saw, began tending to the fragile girl, who, in her desperate state, was still talking. When rescue worker Wayne Eells asked for her name, she replied, "Megan O'Rourke." Then she asked if they had found her friend. "Who's your friend?" Eells asked. She answered, "Melissa Walbridge." Then, in horrific pain and struggling to breathe, she asked the EMT if he could wait to ask her more questions.

Two Essex police officers who had been dispatched to the scene, Michael Bolduc and Gary Taylor, raced through the park to find Melissa. The hope was that she might be wandering around, injured and disoriented, as Megan had been about an hour before.

They took off on parallel paths through the woods. In time, Bolduc encountered a man with a briefcase walking toward him, likely, he thought, an employee from nearby IBM. When he asked the man whether he'd seen anyone coming out of the woods, the man said he hadn't but made Bolduc aware of a smaller path that went deeper into the woods to a place he'd seen kids in the past. Bolduc explored the smaller path. It wasn't long before he came to a place where the ground and greenery looked disturbed. Beyond this area, Bolduc noticed a clearing. While making his way through the branches that tore at his clothing, he found what he was looking for: a hideaway, a spot where someone had hunkered down. He saw two foam mattresses, mildewed and flecked with dirt, and around those, old cigarette butts and shreds of notebook paper. Bolduc took in the scene, his eyes scanning. From under one of the mattresses peeked a small arm and the top of a head. His voice resonated in the damp air, "I found her!" Then he shouted again, his voice carrying in the silence of the woods, "I found her!"

Detective Taylor paused, staring through the dense thicket to gauge the other officer's location. Then he took off, making his way to the clearing. When he got there, Bolduc was kneeling, holding the corner of a grimy mattress. Without looking up, he uttered the words, "She's dead."

Melissa was found lying face down, her head against a toppled, decaying tree. She had been gagged with a sock, and her wrists were bound. Her hands appeared to be grasping, a pose that let investigators know she'd likely been trying to free herself when she died. There was a pellet gun wound in her back, and X-shaped knife marks had been carved in her chest. She'd been shot through one eye. To Officer Taylor, the scene looked more like something you'd see in New York City, not a community like Essex Junction.

As the call went out through various channels, people from the community and local news reporters began showing up, wanting to catch a glimpse of

The path behind Maple Street Park. *Roger Lewis.*

the grisly scene, but State's Attorney Mark Keller sealed off the woods. As the sky grew dark, crime lab workers and rescue crews ran wires and lights through the trees so the collection of evidence could continue. *Burlington Free Press* reporter Mike Donoghue, who normally had a good rapport with local law enforcement, breached the barricades and was warned to get out or risk arrest. The scene was bloody and the torture inflicted on Melissa while she was alive, apparent. The investigators couldn't fathom an attack like this on two little girls who seemed to them hardly more than babies. The case was a sensitive one for all involved.

At the Medical Center Hospital of Vermont, a ten-person trauma crew, including four thoracic surgeons, had been assembled to work on Megan, whose V-shaped stab wound, perilously close to her heart, was deemed by a doctor to be "life threatening." In addition to this near-fatal wound, Megan suffered scratches, strangulation wounds and a puncture at the side of her neck thought to have been made by a BB gun at close range.

It was the job of Deputy State's Attorney Susan Via to find out who had caused Megan's injuries and the death of her friend Melissa. Local police organizations were hot to bring the girls' attackers to justice but had no idea who they might be. Megan held the key to their arrest. Via entered the operating room to question the girl, whose body, attached to rubber tubes, was still caked in mud. As a doctor patted Megan's hair to soothe her, Via asked her questions that could be answered by raising fingers to mean yes or no. Meanwhile, Robin Hallwodel, an Essex patrol officer, took notes.

Did she know her attackers? No. Were they in a car? No. Did she remember what they looked like? Here, the doctor removed Megan's oxygen mask.

One man was blond, and the other had dark hair and a beard, she said. They were the same men who had been in Maple Street Park a few days prior. At that time, they had chased her.

Armed with more information than they'd had previously, Via hurried from Megan's bedside. Leaving the hospital, she was flagged down by a nurse at the reception desk who was holding the phone out to her. Melissa's mother, Marie Walbridge, was on the line. She wanted to know how Megan was, and she wanted news of her daughter. Via began gently questioning Marie and, learning her husband wasn't home, offered to send an officer to the house. Marie, frantic, declined, threatening to come to the hospital, so Villa had no choice but to tell her Melissa had died.

Running on coffee and fumes, investigators were following every lead they had and calling on every bit of expertise available.

Mark Keller, in recalling those days, told me his deputy, Bob Simpson, was the operation's "thinker." Whenever things got hairy, he'd send Bob, who had a great analytical mind, into a room to look at what they knew so far and think about it. It was Bob who, the day after the murder, told Keller that the Essex Police Department was going to need more phone lines, so Keller called the telephone company. "They had a guy over there in fifteen minutes," Keller said. Later in the week, with hundreds of calls coming in every day, they needed even more lines. Again, they didn't have to wait. The phone company, perhaps knowing what was at stake, had an installation tech there pronto.

Early state police bulletins said the darker-haired suspect was in his forties, maybe early fifties, an unintentional red herring, and the first composite sketches were somewhat off the mark. With help from Meghan, the drawings were fine-tuned, and authorities thought they were the best likenesses they could have.

A thousand pink fliers were distributed in the area, and the killers were put on display for all to see.

Then there was an important tip. Ted White, then the principal of one of the Old North End elementary schools, H.O. Wheeler (now the Integrated Arts Academy), called Essex Police to say the composite sketches looked like

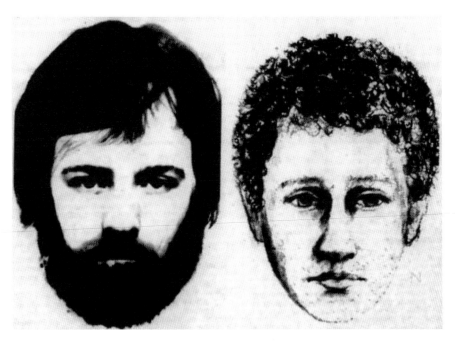

Police sketches of Louis Hamlin and Jamie Savage. *Essex Police Department.*

two former students, Louis Hamlin, sixteen, and Jamie Savage, fifteen. As elementary school students, Hamlin and Savage had grown up mere blocks from the school, Hamlin at 11 Elmwood Avenue and Savage in a small upstairs apartment at 4 Spring Street.

Bob Simpson had the task of looking over the evidence and the leads, scouring the sex offender data base and puzzling out the psychological factors that could cause a particular kind of person to commit that type of crime. It was Bob who sifted through the grab bag of dozens of possible suspects looking for answers. He passed the Savage and Hamlin information on to Keller, telling him they were possible suspects the team might want to focus on. He reminded his boss that Louis Hamlin was not unknown to them. The previous January, Hamlin had been arrested for threatening a woman named Candace Hackett with a knife. In court, the boy had pleaded guilty and had been given a zero- to one-year prison sentence, which was suspended since he was a minor and he'd caused no bodily harm.

The following morning, Ted White called Essex Police yet again. His homeschool coordinator Joyce Hoffman was Hamlin's aunt. She told White she believed the composite sketch looked like Louis. Not long after, a waitress from the Lincoln Inn in Essex, where Jamie Savage worked, visited the Essex

The childhood home of Jamie Savage. *T. Lewis.*

Police Station to report she thought the other composite looked like Jamie Savage. With tips coming in from all over town—in fact, all over the state—it was becoming clear to Essex Police lieutenant Robert Yandow that these two, who came up multiple times from various sources, did indeed deserve a closer look.

Days had gone by with the men who assaulted two little girls and killed one still at large. The community was in a state of grief, disbelief and panic. In Melissa's neighborhood, people couldn't get the murder out of their minds. Melissa was described by teachers and neighbors as a polite child, "well-balanced," a cute kid with freckles across her nose who made cards with pens and markers to advertise her babysitting services. One couple, Michael and Patty Garvey, had taken her up on her entrepreneurial venture. Patty Garvey told *Burlington Free Press* reporters Mike Donoghue and Joe Mahoney that Melissa was "the epitome of innocence," and Michael Garvey revealed that when he heard what had happened to the friendly, petite little girl he "cried for half an hour."

Taking another step toward closing in on Hamlin and Savage, police contacted Louis's older brother John, who was being housed in foster care. After picking up Jamie's brother Rene on an outstanding charge, the police began to question the two. Rene wasn't too keen on cooperating, but John led police on a tour of some of Louis's favorite haunts, including a makeshift cabin at the city dump. Police hoped to find evidence there, but all they found were soggy girlie magazines.

It took just over a week to corner Jamie and Louie. In the wee hours of Thursday, May 21, the teens were picked up on a nontestimonial identification order, a court order to be photographed that had been obtained from Judge Edward Costello, at about 11:00 p.m. at Costello's home address. They were driven to the state police offices to have their pictures taken.

As Louis went off alone in a patrol car, Mary Hamlin, his mother, was worried. Just that morning, she'd told her son's probation officer and the family pediatrician that she had suspicions about Louis. Now, she wondered if she'd done the right thing.

Her husband, Butch, was working the night shift at Burlington's Koffee Kup bakery. While Mary waited for her mother-in-law to arrive to watch her remaining children, she grew more anxious.

Jamie Savage was picked up at the Gaines Court home of Cathy Bailey, the friend his family was living with at the time. As he made ready to leave with the officers, his mother and stepfather, Janet and Bernie Lefebre, told him they would not be far behind.

The press, eager to get their story, had been carefully following the movements of people from Keller's office and the police. When Mike Donoghue from the *Burlington Free Press* saw that Robbie Yandow had signed off as being at Judge Costello's house late in the evening, he was suspicious. He expressed his feeling that something was going on to Keller, who told him nothing was happening. In reality, Keller and the entire team were hiding the fact that the operation was switching headquarters, as they figured it was best to bring these kids in on the down-low. If they hadn't committed the crimes, there was no point in subjecting them to negative notoriety that could affect their entire lives.

As it turns out, they needn't have worried. Later that morning, Megan identified them both from photographic lineups conducted in her hospital room. The two teenagers were arrested. When Megan found out the police had them, she cried.

While in custody and being questioned by police, Jamie Savage changed his story multiple times, but ultimately, he claimed it was his friend who had killed Melissa Walbridge. Savage, who was not yet sixteen, could not be tried as an adult, so murder charges were brought against only Louis Hamlin III.

In the period before the trial, both Hamlin and Savage were incarcerated, but their situations were like night and day. Jamie, who wasn't in jail, was being supervised, but his days were spent playing games like ping-pong. Louis spent his time in isolation, surrounded by four bare walls with only books to pass the time.

Vermonters weren't happy that, even though Savage had participated in the crime, as a fifteen-year-old, he could not be prosecuted. A law passed in 1968 prevented juveniles from being tried in criminal court. He would continue to be detained as a juvenile and then set free with his record wiped clean on his eighteenth birthday.

In response to a huge public outcry, Governor Richard Snelling called a special session of the Vermont legislature to change the rules of the state's juvenile justice system. The new law would give judges discretion to bring to trial any child over the age of ten. Several years after the murder of Melissa Walbridge, the state opened a thirty-bed facility in Essex called Woodside Juvenile Rehabilitation Center. Until 2020, when the center was closed, it was the state's only locked facility for offenders under eighteen. Vermont now finds itself short on space for housing these juveniles, who have lately been placed in adult facilities.

Because of the publicity surrounding the Hamlin trial, the proceedings were moved to Woodstock, Vermont, where his defense team did their best to create reasonable doubt. In an about-face before the start of the trial, Savage had confessed to the murder, saying he killed Melissa and, in a frenzy, had tried to kill Megan as well. But Savage couldn't be tried, so the prosecution, knowing this, painted him as being too stupid to have been the ringleader, with Mark Keller calling him "dumber than four cords of wood."

On May 14, 1982, after just four hours of deliberation, Louis Hamlin was found guilty of first-degree murder and aggravated sexual assault.

At his sentencing, Hamlin, who had recently turned seventeen, told those assembled in the courtroom that he was sorry and that he had recently become a born-again Christian. He asked not for his freedom but for help, saying, "The psychiatrists have said there's no hope for me. They're wrong, and I know it." He was sentenced to forty-five years to life and would not be eligible for parole for thirty years.

While there was never an excuse for what Louis Hamlin had done, there may have been an explanation. After he was arrested, police, of course, obtained a search warrant for his home. When they got there, his father, Louis Hamlin II, refused to let them in a room he'd created, telling them it was his private space and not part of the search warrant. Officers who were sent to execute the warrant called Mark Keller, informing him Hamlin wouldn't grant them access and asking how they should proceed. "Kick the f*cking door down." he told them. When they got inside the space at 11 Elmwood Avenue, they found a house of horrors, featuring pornographic photographs of Louis Hamlin's fifteen-year-old sister that the elder Hamlin

The former Elmwood Avenue home of Louis Hamlin. *Roger Lewis.*

had taken. It was revealed he'd been molesting his daughter since she was four and had told her she'd have to submit only until she turned eighteen. Louis Hamlin and his older brother were also molested by their father and their uncle, which may have contributed not only to his treatment of Megan and Melissa but also to his assault on his thirteen-year-old sister two days before his fifteenth birthday.

Louis "Butch" Hamlin II ended up with a prison sentence of six to fifteen years. A requirement of his incarceration was an experimental treatment program for sex offenders at the Vermont State Hospital in Waterbury. He sued in protest. Ten years after he was released from prison, Butch Hamlin made the news again. In 2019, during a sweep by local, state and federal officials, it was discovered that he was in possession of child pornography. In 2021, the seventy-seven-year-old pleaded guilty to one count of knowingly producing child pornography with intent to distribute. As of this writing he's serving out a five-year prison term.

14

THE MURDER MART

The Champlain Farms store on the corner of Main Street and South Winooski Avenue has long been a fixture in downtown Burlington. You can get gas, cigarettes, snacks and various sundries there. And if you talk to the right person, they might even be able to tell you how the store got its macabre nickname.

Around 6:00 p.m. on November 29, 1986, two men walked into the Champlain Farms store hoping to buy cigarettes, but there was nobody there to assist them. Their search for a clerk revealed a shocking scene: twenty-six-year-old Kimberly Giroux of South Burlington, whose parents had bought the business about a year earlier, was dead in the store office. She'd been physically assaulted, her skull crushed by a fire extinguisher found lying next to her body. She'd also been stabbed. The men, who did not wish to be identified, went to alert police. Another customer who entered the store, Bill Dupre, saw a second victim, identified as eighteen-year-old Richard Aiken of Burlington, sprawled out on the floor in the walk-in cooler. Aiken, who had serious head trauma, was in critical condition. He was given aid at the scene and taken to the Medical Center Hospital, where he later died from his injuries.

Police were all over the scene, and it didn't take long to find a motive. Kimberly had been found where the store's money was kept. Whoever had brutally beaten and robbed her fled with about $2,200.

All over town, people were shaken. They had every right to be. At the time, I lived close to Burlington's downtown area and worked in the local

The "Murder Mart" on Main Street in Burlington. *Roger Lewis.*

mall, then called Burlington Square, at a candy store called Sweet Dreams. I always felt like I knew fairly well and could be at ease with other people who worked in the area. I assumed I was safe leaving the store to make a bank deposit when the mall closed at 9:00 p.m., but now, I wasn't so sure. It was hard for me to grasp that two people had been killed early on a Saturday evening at a corner store so close to the Church Street Marketplace—so close to my place of work.

Just imagine how I felt when I found out I knew the murderer.

In the aftermath, across Chittenden County, store owners were beefing up their security and telling employees not to argue with robbers. "Let the cash go," they said. Police continued their investigation into the next week, scouring the ground from rooftops, writing down license plate numbers and searching nearby yards. Evidence from the scene had gone to the state lab for analysis or to the FBI.

By December 4, Burlington Police had narrowed down the time of the murders to between 5:30 p.m. and 5:58 p.m.

They'd recovered at least one murder weapon, and they had prints. Chief Kevin Scully said his team were working out several "case scenarios" and that they weren't ruling out professionals, ex-employees or people who held a grudge against the owners. On December 5, they took their suspect into custody. Twenty-nine-year-old Samuel Wright Jr. worked less than a block from the scene of the murder. Police had matched his fingerprints to the ones they lifted from the fire extinguisher, and footprints that were found on the floor next to Kimberly Giroux's body matched the tread from Wright's sneaker. Eyewitness accounts said a "Hispanic-looking man" fitting Wright's description, with black, wavy hair and glasses, was seen talking to Kimberly about an hour before she died.

At his arraignment, Wright pleaded not guilty. Judge Linda Leavitt set his bail at $50,000. Without that kind of money, Wright, who had worked washing dishes at the popular Nectar's restaurant, was detained at the Chittenden Community Correctional Center, a place whose tongue-in-cheek nickname, "the Four Cs," make it sound decidedly tropical and a lot more fun than it actually is.

Hearing of Sam's arrest for the murder, I was more than a little spooked. I'd first met him at the Burlington Square Mall, where he'd worked at the bakery right next door to Sweet Dreams. He was easygoing and even charming in a brash sort of way and an expert at the "humble brag" before it had a name.

When Sam worked at the bakery it was suspected but never proved that he had "special" products you could buy, and that he kept them in the kitchen where employees hung their coats. Kids who worked for me joked about how, sometimes, while they were waiting to buy coffee or a muffin, another customer would hand Sam cash that was folded up and leave the counter with a little white bakery bag that looked like it held nothing at all. This is conjecture, but in light of what we'd later learn, it's definitely something to think about.

Samuel Wright Jr. was born in West Germany, but like his father, he was a legal citizen of Bermuda. Court records from Montreal showed he had been arrested a slew of times for a variety of offenses (auto theft and narcotics to name a few). He served two years in jail, got out and then, six months later, was arrested for leaving the scene of an accident, for which he served another two weeks. He was a familiar face in Burlington, a place he'd lived for about six years. He also had priors in Vermont, and members of the local police department knew him on sight. Kimberly's parents knew him, too. He was a regular at the store, and her mother, Betty Giroux, recalled after he was rounded up that only a few weeks before, knowing he had a baby, she'd pointed out that diapers were on sale.

Samuel Wright Jr. in custody. *WCAX-TV.*

During the pretrial phase, in August 1987, it was ruled that the police had violated the defendant's right to a lawyer before making statements, a win for the defense. Wright also got a "gimme" when the contents of his personal diary, in which he wrote that he planned to kill someone, were found inadmissible in court.

Wright's trial was scheduled to begin on October 19, 1987, but the defense requested more time and got it. Meanwhile, a monkey wrench was thrown into the works for the prosecution when a key member of their team, Deputy State's Attorney Karen Shingler, was processed for driving while intoxicated and suspended from her job without pay.

During preliminary hearings, which began just a few days before Christmas that year, prosecutors knew they had to hit the ground running. Before the judge, they posed that Wright was in the Champlain Farms store looking for money to purchase weed and cocaine. They had testimony from a witness named Steven Vuley of Burlington that Wright had visited his house with a large amount of cash about an hour after the murder. Another man, Preston Layton, said that later that evening, he witnessed Wright mainlining cocaine.

In addition to the witness testimony, there was another score for the prosecution when Judge Leavitt allowed into evidence three color photographs of Kimberly Giroux's dead body lying on the floor in the store's office. The defense claimed the photographs' graphic nature would unduly influence the jury, but the prosecution knew the color pictures were important, since they illustrated how Wright had, allegedly, sprayed foam around the office in the hopes of obscuring evidence. Leavitt also allowed for testimony from a former Champlain Farms employee, Robert Williams, who said Wright had mentioned to him the store would be "an easy hit" and tried to talk him into helping him rob it.

Early in the case, Wright's wife, Barbara, told police that her husband had given her cash and told her to "go buy a TV." She also answered their questions about whether she thought her husband had committed the murder. Public defender Jerry Schwartz requested this information be excluded from her testimony, citing spousal privilege. The judge agreed but ruled that the prosecution could ask other questions—about Wright's conduct and demeanor the night of the murder, the condition of his hands and whether he appeared to be under the influence of cocaine.

As it turns out, Barbara had shown investigators who visited her home a knife set. It was missing a six-inch knife. This information eventually led to an argument between the defense and prosecution over a piece of evidence they didn't even have.

Michael McGowan, a former detective with the BPD and now an FBI agent, was able to track down an identical knife set at a Woolworths store in St. Albans, and a tool marks expert with the Vermont State Police examined it, finding that the grooves in the blade that was missing from the Wright's knife set perfectly matched nicks on a ring Kimberly Giroux was wearing while she defended her life. The defense countered this by saying that "waving a knife around" when it wasn't the murder weapon was extremely prejudicial.

But the judge weighed in that though the knife itself would probably not be admitted into evidence, the forensic findings could likely be introduced anyway.

In the end, the trial was held not in Burlington but in Barre. As it was ongoing, Karen Shingler made a visit to the Northwest Regional Correctional Facility. During the visit, she was allowed to enter Wright's cell while he was absent. His defense team took exception to the visit. Attorney Schwartz called it an "escapade," said it violated his client's rights. He called for a dismissal. The judge rejected the request but reminded Shingler that files she obtained on Wright while visiting the jail had to be made available to the defense.

The defense team knew they needed to create reasonable doubt. During their attempt to do so, there was a claim made by public defender W. Gilbert

Livingston that it wasn't Wright but the victim's ex-boyfriend, a former store employee named Dominic Ladue, who killed Kimberly. Livingston suggested Ladue was angry at the victim's decision to have an abortion. He pressed for access to the Kimberly's medical records. After a review of the documents in the judge's chambers, a decision was made by the court to not disclose them, as they would not be helpful to the defense. It was a great smoke-and-mirrors attempt, but police had already taken the time to rule out Ladue as a suspect. He had an alibi, and after all, it was Wright's fingerprints on the fire extinguisher and his sneaker print in the office.

Wright attended all court proceedings looking well-groomed and impeccably dressed, usually in a sport coat and tie. He wasn't fidgety; in fact, he seemed almost calm, often stroking his mustache or bending his head to scribble a few notes.

The prosecution continued to paint him as a user and abuser of drugs, bringing in witnesses who testified that on the night of the murder he'd shown up at the home of a dealer, his pockets stuffed with cash and paid off a debt for cocaine he'd fronted some time before. He then allegedly began handing out $10 bills to children who lived in the apartment "like he was dealing cards." He also bought more cocaine. The roughly $2,200 he stole after bludgeoning and stabbing Kimberly Giroux was the "gift" that kept on giving. In addition to a new TV, he bought Barbara an amethyst ring.

On Monday, January 11, it was finally Wright's turn to testify. He claimed that on the night of the murder, around 5:00 p.m., he made his first stop at Champlain Farms, where he spoke to Richard Aiken, who wanted to buy some hashish. Wright told him he'd return later, but when he did, he saw the bloody aftermath and fled. He said he thought with his priors, the police wouldn't buy that he had nothing to do with the crime. He cited his fear of a confrontation with Burlington Police detective Emmet Helrich, whom he'd burned in an undercover drug operation just a few weeks before by fleeing with a wire and $100 Helrich had given him. He explained away his prints on the fire extinguisher by saying because the office was dark, he had to move it out of the way to get a better look at the victim. He told the court the testimony from witnesses at the drug house he visited that described him as having rolls of cash in mostly small bills wasn't true. When prosecutor Shingler asked if the witnesses were liars, Wright shrugged, "If you say so."

The jury began their deliberations in the Wright trial on January 13, 1988. After being sequestered for just six and a half hours, they returned their verdict, which was read at 7:40 p.m. in front of John and Darlene Walker,

Richard Aiken, the second victim in the "Murder Mart" slaying. *Mount Abraham UHS Aerie.*

Richard Aiken's mother and stepfather, and his sister, Laurie. Wright's wife, Barbara, and his parents, who'd been present for most of the trial, had gone home earlier in the day. Giroux's parents, James and Betty, were also absent when Wright was found guilty of first-degree murder in the killing of Kimberly Giroux.

While he was awaiting sentencing, Wright lodged a complaint that he'd been given inadequate legal counsel. He moved to have his public defenders withdrawn from the case, asking Judge Leavitt to appoint a replacement. Prosecutor Kevin Bradley argued against the motion, saying Wright was entitled to competent counsel but not the counsel of his choice. The motion was denied.

By the day of his sentencing, April 8, Wright was still proclaiming his innocence. Giroux's mother, speaking to the court, told how Kimberly's daughter, just four years old at the time of her mother's murder had said, "I wish my mom could visit me for just one day and then go back to heaven." She added that she and her husband thought Wright should go to prison for the rest of his life. "I hate to be this way, a tooth for a tooth," she said, "but he took my daughter away." Prosecutor Bradley told the court what happened at Champlain Farms the night Wright took Kimberly's life was "inhuman madness."

Citing Wright's drug use and a violent history that included assaults on his wife, Bradley and Wright's probation officer suggested Wright receive a sentence of seventy-five years in prison. In the end, he was sentenced to what was believed to be the longest jail term ever set out by a Vermont court—sixty years to life. Giroux's mother said, when asked about the verdict, "It will never bring Kim back, but at least I have the satisfaction the man who did it is going to be punished."

While it's always been assumed that eighteen-year-old Richard Aiken was Wright's second victim, there was never anything more than circumstantial evidence to support the theory, so he was never charged with his murder. Despite Wright's claim that he was looking for drugs for the teen, Aiken's shift was set to end just six minutes after he was killed on that Thanksgiving weekend. It's possible Wright was waiting for Giroux to be working alone, an easy target, and simply miscalculated.

For a time, Aiken's murder was listed on the Vermont State Police website as "unsolved," but it's no longer there. There must be a statute of limitations on how long you can ignore something that, despite the technicalities, is plain for all to see.

15

AS SEEN ON COURT TV

Do you Reddit? If you're not familiar, Reddit is an online "network of communities where people can dive into their interests, hobbies and passions." I started taking breaks in the Reddit world back in 2020 and stumbled on a subreddit called, AITA (Google it). It's full of examples of situations that bring out the worst in humanity, including an endless supply of self-centered brides who drone on about people who spoil their wedding day, a day that should be perfect, unicorn-dusted and all about them. It's gotten to the point that I think I'll whack myself with an enormous unity candle if I have to read one more post about a bride's expectations, because marriages should be about the couple, *their* love and *their* dreams for the future.

I realize it doesn't always work out that way. It surely didn't for Michael Durenleau.

On July 12, 1985, around 10:00 p.m., Michael John Durenleau and his wife, Rebecca Starr Durenleau, or Becky, as she was called, left Veronica's Tavern, a popular watering hole near the Five Corners in Essex Junction, and were getting into their car when, according to Rebecca, an unknown assailant jumped from the tall grass near the vehicle and bludgeoned and stabbed Michael before fleeing into the woods. She said the suspect, who was between five foot, three inches, and five foot, six inches tall, was wearing dark clothing and didn't issue any commands or demand their wallets. She couldn't tell whether the individual who attacked her spouse was a man or a woman (though later investigators would determine, based on the strength

The senior class photograph of Rebecca Dumont (Durenleau). *From the Swanton High School Log.*

needed to inflict the head wounds her husband sustained, whoever had struck the blows had been a man). The attack had lasted mere seconds, after which Rebecca said she went for help.

Her husband, critically injured, was rushed from the scene to the Medical Center Hospital in Burlington, where he died on the operating table.

When interviewed about the incident, Veronica's owner, Judy Varriccione, said the couple, who she'd never seen before, came in for one beer and were in her place less than half an hour. She also offered that patrons who visited her bar at night normally avoided the dark lot where the two had parked. Even in the daytime, the spot, which was next to the railroad tracks and the lumberyard and dotted with broken down cars and debris, wasn't exactly welcoming. She was puzzled about why the Durenleaus had parked their car so far from the tavern when there were vacant spaces closer to the entrance.

It might not have made sense to Varriccione, but to people who knew the couple, the picture came together pretty quickly. Rebecca had a rather poorly kept secret: she no longer had any use for her husband. In fact, she'd told a friend that she'd have a lot fewer problems if her husband was dead.

Before he died, Michael "Alky" Durenleau was a former national guardsman and a more than fifteen-year employee of the Harrison Construction Company. Rebecca was employed as an office manager. The couple, part of a large extended family, had been sweethearts since their teens and had been married for nearly fourteen years. They had two children, Jason and Jennifer, creating the perfect nuclear family.

But life for the two wasn't all it seemed, because Rebecca had taken a lover, a man named Harmon Olmstead.

By August 1984, Rebecca had filed for divorce from Michael, but the road to divorce can be messy and long. It seemed to Becky there was no clear path for her and Olmstead to be together without losing the house she shared with Michael and risking custody of her minor children, which she couldn't see happening. She dropped the divorce proceedings, and she and Michael endured an on-and-off-again relationship while she continued to pursue her affair with Olmstead. It was a precarious time. A witness would later testify that Becky secretly allowed Olmstead to be around her kids while using the assumed name "Richard Gadbois," which was actually the name of Harmon's lawyer. Olmstead and Michael had at least one face-to-face altercation. By the spring of 1985, it appeared to Michael the couple had reconciled, but he was being deceived; Becky told her mother she was going through with the divorce. Not only was she still seeing Olmstead, but she also wasn't being shy about it, appearing with him at a very public Fourth of July party that was held approximately one week before her husband's murder. During one of the couple's trysts Becky allegedly told her lover that unless he "proved himself" to her she would resume sexual relations with her husband. Later, there was much speculation about the phrase, its timing and what exactly it meant.

The couple's outing to Veronica's was planned several days in advance. On the evening of July 12, Michael and Becky left their home in Swanton and headed to Essex Junction.

Rebecca was driving. She parked the car, nose out, in the derelict lot at approximately 9:30 p.m.

Once inside Veronica's, they found a vacant table right away. But their visit was short-lived. For whatever reason, they headed back to their car fifteen to twenty minutes after they arrived. Rebecca again headed for the driver's seat. The attack commenced. Becky would later say she heard Michael utter as it was happening, "I've had enough!"

It's known that she ran back to the bar and shouted that her husband had been "hit" but did not immediately give patrons his location. They began running out the door and into the street, assuming she meant he'd been hit by a car. Becky came out of the bar to redirect them. She followed the crowd to the scene, standing some distance away as strangers attempted to revive her husband, who was close to death.

There was no theft, no injury to Becky and no killer in sight.

But man, oh, man, there was plenty of talk, and the rumor mill contributed to the suspicions held by authorities. Michael's family expected swift justice. Their loved one had no criminal associates, and it was assumed he'd come to his death through no fault of his own. Essex police had a suspect early on, and though the individual wasn't named, most people believed they knew who it was. Time went by with no charges filed. Rebecca, uncharacteristically, wasn't talking. She referred all questions regarding the case to her attorney.

Years dragged on with no movement in the case. In a weird turn of events, it was discovered that the box containing the original investigative files pertaining to Michael Durenleau's murder had disappeared. Fortunately, the materials were able to be reconstructed by Essex and state police using photocopies.

Park Place Tavern, the location of the old Veronica's Tavern. *Roger Lewis.*

None of this seemed to affect Rebecca. With her husband out of the picture, she used the money from his life insurance policy to buy land belonging to Harmon Olmstead. The two had a new house built on the property and moved into it together in 1989.

It must have felt to Rebecca that life had turned out exactly the way she'd hoped—that is, until September 1991, when she was charged with her husband's murder.

A grand jury was convened and found probable cause to convict her. State's Attorney William Sorrell offered that Olmstead did "willfully, deliberately, with premeditation and with malice aforethought, kill and murder Michael Durenleau." But they had no evidence beyond hearsay to pin the crime on Rebecca's lover. Instead, they had to go after Rebecca, the perceived mastermind behind the killing.

Rebecca's attorney, Peter Langrock, argued the case against his client should be dropped, saying the state had not been aggressive enough in filing charges against Harmon Olmstead, the alleged killer. He admitted his client "concedes that Harmon Olmstead may be the suspect" but noted that because there wasn't enough evidence to charge *him*, the state also lacked enough cause in charging Rebecca with helping him. Judge Matthew Katz refused to drop the charges.

The stage was set for a tense and emotional trial, with families on both sides present for the testimony. Adding to the sensationalism was the fact that it was being broadcast by the national cable network Court TV.

Dr. Eleanor McQuillen took the stand, telling the gallery that any of the four injuries Michael Durenleau had sustained the evening of his death could have killed him. The five-foot-two-inch-tall, 135-pound victim had been clubbed twice in the head and stabbed twice through the heart. His autopsy showed he had a cut on one of his fingers, a defense wound. McQuillen believed Michael was attacked by not one individual but two and that at least one of the stab wounds was inflicted before he was struck over the head. She told the court that one person would not have been able to switch weapons so quickly and also mentioned that the injuries he sustained would have caused the victim to collapse in a heap, not lie on his back in the position the men who went to his aid described.

Essex Police lieutenant Robin Hollwedel testified that when questioned at the crime scene, Rebecca became obviously more agitated and was eventually unresponsive. But as the medical examiner listed her dead husband's injuries in detail, she showed no emotion.

Interesting but not surprising was the fact that Harmon Olmstead was a no-show at court the first day, and he pleaded the fifth when he finally did show. Those watching learned that Olmstead had fled to Oregon for a period after Michael's death, something police learned about from his mother, who said her son had conferred with a lawyer a few days after the crime and, on his advice, taken an unscheduled trip to visit relatives. They also heard from Brenda Donna, the woman Olmstead was married to at the time of the killing. She'd found out about the affair late, she said, only about ten days before Michael Durenleau died. She told the court that within a month of the killing, her husband had moved out of the house and filed for divorce.

The jury heard from Rebecca Durenleau's own mother that her daughter had recounted to her several conflicts between her husband and lover, including an argument at a St. Albans bar called the Outpost. Rebecca allegedly said Olmstead had warned Michael, "I'll get you sooner or later."

Later in the trial, an acquaintance of Rebecca's, Ellen Smith of Sheldon, Vermont, testified that during a visit to her home, Rebecca had told her Olmstead had called her after Michael was killed and told her he had "proven himself." And of course, there was no way prosecutors would not offer the revelation of Rebecca's supposed forgery of Michael's life insurance application and the payout she'd received of more than $90,000.

Speaking of money, there was talk of a witness who, on the night of the murder, had seen Olmstead with Rebecca's brother Raymond Dumont. It was also claimed that Dumont was the recipient of substantial bank transfers from Rebecca that were made after Michael's murder, including a check for $10,000, on which she'd written, "Happy Birthday." State police would later say the check was actually for $20,000. Dumont, however, had an alibi for the night of the murder: a woman who claimed he'd been with her.

Another fascinating tidbit that emerged was that Becky had taken a lie detector test the day after the murder and passed. Afterward, police learned she'd taken sedatives beforehand. They asked her to retake the test. She refused, making findings of her innocence or guilt inconclusive.

On Sunday, August 30, the jury ruled that Rebecca Durenleau had aided her lover Harmon Olmstead in the murder of her husband, Michael Durenleau. One by one, jury members uttered the word "guilty." Before they could finish, Rebecca put her head down and began to sob, collapsing on the floor. Officers and her family members gathered around her. Complaining of chest pains, she was removed from the courtroom and taken to the Medical Center Hospital for observation. With her bail revoked by Judge Katz, the forty-year-old mother of two was later taken to the Chittenden Community Correctional Center.

Interviewed after the trial concluded, one of the jurors, Lloyd Gilbert of Milton, said the decision "was not based on any one thing. It seemed to tie itself together, most of it, by itself."

In October, just a few months after this decision was reached, there was a motion for appeal, with Langrock saying the state hadn't submitted enough evidence. Judge Katz took these arguments under advisement.

In January, Katz heard arguments for a new trial. Knowing that both the victims' and the defendants' families would again be present and that the stakes would higher than before, he ordered heightened security. Lawyers, reporters and spectators were subject to pat-downs before entering the courtroom. During the hearing, Langrock presented information that a piece of evidence, a sledgehammer identified as one of the weapons used to kill Michael Durenleau, had been lost or destroyed before the trial began. He posed that the murder weapon could as easily have been a railroad switch handle found near the scene instead of a tool brought there by the defendant or her boyfriend. Scot Kline, the new state's attorney, agreed the weapon had been lost in the interim period between the murder and the trial but countered, "Where there is a failure to preserve evidence, the burden is on the defense to demonstrate bad faith [on the part of the state]," which had not been done.

On January 6, Judge Katz made his ruling. Becky's conviction would stand. There would be no new trial.

On March 22, 1993, Rebecca Durenleau, still protesting her innocence, was sentenced to thirty-five years to life in prison. William Sorrell, who was serving at the time as Vermont's secretary of administration, told the court the defendant's actions were "the epitome of a premeditated, cold blooded murderer….Mrs. Durenleau is a murderer." Durenleau screamed back at him, "I am not a murderer!" Her attorney reached out to hold her back.

Michael's sister Rachel Boucher said to Rebecca in a statement from the family, "We believe you are a sick and twisted person. How you have been able to live with yourself is beyond my understanding."

It seemed Rachel and the rest of Michael's family might finally get the closure they were hoping for. But in May 1994, a little more than a year after Rebecca's sentencing, Langrock brought her appeal to the Vermont Supreme Court, arguing again that the state's case had too many flaws.

One of the justices, Judge James Morse, asked Rosemary Hull of the state's attorney's office why Olmstead, who was sitting in the courtroom, had never been charged. "You convinced a jury that he was guilty of first-degree murder beyond a reasonable doubt in her case," he said. "Why not do it over again?"

Amid the appeal, Rebecca's daughter, Jennifer, was making plans to marry. Rebecca had already missed her son's high school graduation (the Department of Corrections had agreed to let her go but decided against it at the last minute), and she wanted to attend the July nuptials. Attorney Langrock said two guards from the correctional facility had volunteered their time should Rebecca be allowed to go to the wedding, which was being held at the American Legion in St. Albans. He said it would be "tragic" if she could not be there, causing Rachel Boucher to offer that her brother's murder was the real tragedy. Since he was dead, he couldn't be there to give his daughter away.

Deputy State's Attorney Pamela Hall Johnson told Judge Katz that releasing Rebecca would send the wrong message. Katz, in a nutshell, said incarcerated people do miss out on family events. He denied the request; ditto the Department of Corrections, which confirmed the day before the wedding, "She won't be going anywhere."

Finally, on September 30, 1994, there was a bombshell from the Vermont Supreme Court. In a rare move for a murder case, the justices overturned Rebecca's verdict. In their opinion, the jury had insufficient evidence to convict her. By ordering a judgement of acquittal, the court ensured there would be no retrial. Rebecca Durenleau was a free woman.

Jurors who'd delivered the previous verdict were stunned. Doris Safford of Colchester was quoted as saying, "I couldn't believe it. I was flabbergasted." And Jennifer Coleman of Shelburne said, "I think it's kind of a kick in the butt....I still stand by the verdict."

These days, Rebecca Durenleau, who was remarried in 1995 to a man who wasn't Harmon Olmstead, goes by a different surname and lives in another state. Having made my way through her story, I'm at a loss at how the whole thing shook down. In fact, to borrow the words of Doris Safford, I'm "flabbergasted."

16

THE CHRISTMAS PARTY KILLER

In the '90s there were a slew of spots in Vermont's Queen City where you could hold a decent company function, but the most popular place had to be the Radisson Hotel overlooking Burlington's waterfront. The Radisson had the space and staff to handle conventions, weddings, proms—what have you. And it was the Radisson that Mary Yoh's employers at Williston's Marriott Residence Hotel chose for their holiday party on December 19, 1997.

Mary Yoh, a petite blonde with sky-blue eyes, was born in Connecticut to Louis and Sharon Longo. She and her sisters grew up mostly in the New London, Connecticut area, but the family eventually relocated to Vermont, a place they knew well. They were a tight-knit bunch—more so when their parents died. The youngest sister, Michelle Sicely, told me it fell to Mary to do the mothering. She doted not just on her siblings but on their kids as well and was a favorite among her nieces and nephews.

Mary was a mother of three. She lost one child, a daughter named Misty, to a tragic accident, and had a tattoo with the girl's name on her upper chest. She also had tattoos with the names of her other two kids, a boy named Dale and a girl named Sandy.

Twice divorced, she met Yoh in 1994. He gave her the nickname "Winkie." They were married two years later, even though the family had their doubts about the relationship. One of Mary's sisters, Terry Raymond, said she had a bad feeling about Yoh the first time she met him. Her instincts were on target. The foul-mouthed, bad-tempered Yoh was an abuser who always had

A young Miriam "Mary" Yoh poses holding her daughter in a generational photograph. *Michelle Sicely.*

to have his way. He would punch Mary and kick her, and she spent much of her time married to him covered in bruises. Her sisters recalled a violent beating he gave her once on the night before Thanksgiving. In early 1997, he even stole $2,500 and her car from her before driving to Pennsylvania, where he was picked up and jailed on outstanding charges. From jail, he wrote he'd been missing her, saying, "I just cannot forget all the little tender things we used to say to each other." But in the same letter, he demanded she tell him whether she'd been faithful to him during his incarceration. But it didn't matter what Herman did, Terry said, Mary always went back to him.

At the party on December 19, coworkers couldn't help but notice that Mary and Herman weren't getting along. Eventually, the two left the group, heading to room 537. They'd booked it so they could enjoy the evening without worrying about driving home, but on that night, there was not much enjoyment to be had.

Once upstairs, they began to argue—loudly. Lee Hamilton, a seventeen-year-old hockey player from Massachusetts, was in the room next door and later told police he heard sounds of crying and fighting from room 537

Miriam "Mary" Yoh (*right*) celebrates a special occasion. *Michelle Sicely.*

around 11:45 p.m. There was a loud scream not long after, and a woman's voice shouted, "You have to stop! Stop! You are hurting me!"

As the boy turned down the TV to better hear what was going on, his mother came back into the room. She told her son to turn up the TV and go to bed. By the time she went to bed at about 1:00 a.m., everything was quiet. It was eventually revealed that two other hockey players had heard the screaming and banging and went to the Yoh's room to check on the couple. But there was a "Do Not Disturb" sign on the door.

The next morning, around 7:00 a.m., Herman called Mary's boss, Jay Parizo, saying she wasn't well and wouldn't be coming in that day. Parizo said Yoh told him she was "hugging the porcelain toilet," saying, "You know how it is when you've had too much to drink." Mary never went back to work.

She was expected at a family Christmas party, as she never missed celebrating with her sisters, but she never showed. They thought she might have gotten sidetracked. They knew she and her husband liked to drink. But as weeks went by with no word from her, they contacted the police. They were told officers would keep an eye out, but with no evidence of foul play, no official steps were taken. "When a man and a woman aren't seen for six weeks, there is no law against it," State Police Detective Lieutenant Clayton Perkins said at the time.

Mary's sisters, determined to find her, began creating and distributing missing person fliers.

Weeks later, nearly three months after the holiday party at the Radisson, Mary's badly decomposed and partially frozen body was found. It was March 7. Two men, Albert Lefevbre and Troy O'Brien, were out hunting wild turkeys near Governor Chittenden Road in Williston when they discovered Mary's body wrapped in a pink bedspread, still dressed in the outfit she'd worn to her company Christmas party.

Now, police were keen to question Yoh—if only they knew where he was. They stressed the fact that there were no arrest warrants in the case and posed that Yoh (who was wanted on warrants for driving while intoxicated, driving with a suspended license and violating conditions of release and who was previously convicted of domestic abuse) might also be a victim of foul play.

On March 10, police went to the apartment on Jasper Mine Road in Colchester that Mary and Herman had shared. They learned that their landlord, absent a rent check from the two, had moved their possessions into storage. Police took the belongings to search for clues as Mary's sisters made her final arrangements.

On March 16, after Vermont State Police informed authorities in Reading, Pennsylvania, that a fugitive from justice was likely in their area, Herman Yoh

Miriam "Mary" Yoh in a quiet moment. *Michelle Sicely.*

was picked up at 8:00 a.m. for driving under the influence and violating his probation. He was taken to Berks County Prison.

In Pennsylvania, he told troopers he had taken Mary home from the party because she was feeling ill from drinking too much. He said he left her in their home the next day, called her workplace and told them she was sick and would not be coming in; he then left to run some errands. He told them that upon returning to the apartment, he discovered Mary was gone. He said he stayed until the next day and then left for Reading, where his ex-wife and children lived. When asked why Mary might have disappeared, he said she had been having a dispute with a Vermont bail bondsman named Shelley Palmer, an old employer of his, intimating Palmer might have something to do with her disappearance.

Yoh was then Mirandaed (read his rights) and charged with first-degree murder. He awaited extradition to Vermont. Two days later, Vermont State Police detectives Dane Shortsleeve and Thomas Nelson arrived at the Pennsylvania State Police Barracks. Yoh was read his rights again and submitted to a taped interview. During the interview, the officers did not reveal they'd found Mary, giving her husband the impression she was still missing (something they wouldn't be able to do today with widespread use of the internet). Yoh stuck to the story he'd told the Pennsylvania troopers. After a few hours of questioning, they sprang the news that his wife had been found, but the revelation did not cause Yoh to change his story.

Eventually, Shortsleeve and Nelson accused Yoh of committing the murder, pointing out inconsistencies between his version of what happened and the physical evidence they had so far. There were blood spatters on the walls of room 537. There were witnesses who had come forward about that night. Mary's autopsy report indicated she'd been beaten and strangled. Yoh kept claiming he had nothing to do with his wife's death, but he was rattled. He told the detectives, "You're trying to trip me up. You get an attorney in here or something." Detective Shortsleeve denied trying to trip him up and asked if he wanted to stop the interview. "Yeah," Yoh said. Shortsleeve asked him why. His recorded answer was, "Because." But Detective Shortsleeve wasn't finished. After several minutes of trying to extract more information the easy way, he was blunt: "You expect to get out of jail before you're ninety years old, you need to tell us. Goes right here on the tape. You're not going to get another opportunity." Yoh wasn't swayed.

One of the Pennsylvania state troopers who had conducted his original interview was charged with driving him back to the prison. From the back seat, Yoh asked him who he thought the Vermont detectives would talk to next. The man said he didn't know, but if it was his investigation, he'd be talking to Yoh's family in Pennsylvania to see if they had any information. Thinking about it, Yoh offered, "If you can keep those guys off my family, I will tell them everything they want to know." The officer returned him to the barracks and let the Vermont detectives know the perp was finally ready to talk.

That's when Yoh's story changed. He admitted to Shortsleeve and Nelson that he and Mary had an argument in the hotel room, which escalated. He said Mary taunted him and threatened to call the police. Yoh (with all his many priors), told the detectives that when Mary reached for the telephone, he simply "blacked out," and when he came to, his wife was dead. He couldn't remember what happened after Mary reached for the telephone. He'd "snapped." He said that afterward, he'd wrapped the dead woman's body in a blanket, carried it to his car and driven to Williston. It was a story that would have its variations, but one thing was certain: Herman Yoh had murdered his wife.

Back in Vermont, he was arraigned. He pleaded not guilty and was held for lack of bail, which was set at $1 million.

In prison and awaiting trial, Yoh managed to acquire a fiancée. Her name was Diane Harakaly, and she was a mother of four from Waterville, Vermont. The two met while she was working as a prison guard at the Chittenden Regional Correctional Center and Yoh was newly incarcerated. Harakaly claimed their relationship was a friendship that blossomed, saying it wasn't until she left her third-shift job at the prison that their relationship grew "more serious." She visited him twice a week. On one of those visits, he proposed, and she accepted. She called him a "kind, respectful man with a good sense of humor."

Herman's trial would reveal even more about his movements the night he killed Mary—and afterward. The cold-blooded killer stated he left the hotel to move their car closer to the exit and carried his wife's diminutive body to it by holding her upright, lifting her from under her arms. He drove with her corpse back to their apartment, left it in the car and then ran errands, going to the post office and then to the local mini mart before calling the Marriott to say Mary was sick and wouldn't be in. He then drove around for two hours before finally dumping Mary's body off and fleeing the state to be with his ex-wife, Paula Yoh, and their two children in Reading. His testimony also included a ridiculous piece of fiction that Shelly Palmer, the local bail bondsman he earlier claimed his wife had bad blood with, had hired two hitmen, who entered their hotel room, knocked him out and killed Mary.

Herman Yoh's prison fiancée, Diane Harakaly, can be seen on the far left of the second row. *Vermont Department of Corrections.*

On October 18, 1999, a jury deliberated for just three hours before convicting Herman Yoh of the first-degree murder of Miriam "Mary" Yoh. He was sentenced to life in prison without parole.

In 2006, he appealed his sentence, calling it "unconstitutional." He argued that his Miranda rights against making self-incriminating statements were violated, and he filed a separate post-conviction relief request in superior court, arguing that his lawyer's counsel was "ineffective." The court upheld his conviction. He would remain in jail.

In October 2009, Mary's sisters were back in court and mad as hell about it. It had been ten years since the initial verdict was handed down. Any closure they'd felt had been short-lived. Her youngest sister, Michelle, said, "We're really upset....We were promised we wouldn't be here."

Yoh had agreed just the year before to stop appealing the case in exchange for a lighter sentence. Instead of life without parole, he got a thirty-year minimum sentence and a chance of release, if conditions were met, in about ten years, a deal approved by Mary's family. Now, after promising not to appeal in *Vermont* courts, Yoh was appealing in federal court.

He didn't stop there. In 2022, he filed another complaint, indicating that the Department of Corrections had violated his rights by failing to develop or implement a plan of treatment that would prepare him for his return to the community. The DOC sought to have the claim dismissed. It provided information that Yoh had scored high on tests that measured his risk of reoffending and continuing a pattern of abuse and said the department "does not believe the current programming officered [*sic*] will address his risk to the community."

The court wasn't buying it. Paraphrasing, the court told the Department of Corrections that according to the statutes and assuming most incarcerated individuals end up back in society, it was incumbent the department to figure it out if it didn't have a current program for Herman Yoh.

The motion to dismiss was denied.

Will we see other appeals? Will Herman Yoh walk the streets of Vermont any time soon?

Only time will tell.

17

WITH A BASEBALL BAT

Have you ever attended a baby shower and found out weeks later that the host was wearing a wire and there were surveillance cameras on the premises in compliance with an undercover drug operation?

It happened to me.

Fortunately, since I don't use drugs or sell drugs, all I had to worry about was whether the local cops viewing the tapes, many of whom I knew, would hear anything inappropriate coming out of my mouth during the course of the festivities. I'm known in my family as a blurter. My social anxiety always makes it worse.

The party was held at the apartment of a woman named Ellen Ducharme, someone I'd known for years.

Godmother to my niece and eventual girlfriend to one of my cousins, you couldn't say we were close, but she was part of a group that was always around.

When I met her, she was just a kid, a pretty teenager with a layered haircut in the style of '80s singer Samantha Fox. She had a great laugh, but even though she was always kind and easygoing, there was a shadow behind Ellen's dark eyes. I always thought that despite her outwardly jovial nature, the girl had some pretty sad stories to tell. Back then, I knew she wasn't an angel, by any means, but it seemed like a lot of the trouble she got into was a result of opportunism—hers or someone else's—or bad habits and a sketchy environment. There were an awful lot of teens and adults who were growing up hard in Burlington's Old North End at that time who I could have said the same thing about.

Ellen was born in Springfield, Vermont, on March 21, 1966, to Ron and Mary Ann Lamphere. In August 1984, she married Charles "Charlie" Ducharme. They were both eighteen, and it's not surprising the marriage didn't last. I knew Charlie before I knew Ellen. He was a neighborhood boy who was always out and about, flashing a smile so big, it was like turning on a light. He was eventually murdered, shot eight times inside his own home by the estranged husband of a woman he was seeing.

In her late teens and early twenties, Ellen was charged with crimes that were usually light on consequence: disorderly conduct, simple assault, violation of probation and retail theft. She left a Hansel and Gretel–like trail of retail thefts in Burlington, South Burlington, Winooski and who knows how many other towns. She was picked up in 1985 for driving with a suspended license and aggravated assault, for which she was released on conditions.

Ellen continued to rack up charges for driving with a suspended license and driving while intoxicated. The "Day in Court" column from 1988 lists a cavalcade of charges, including simple assault, driving while intoxicated, driving while license suspended, two violations of probation and an attempt to allude police officers. She was fined $250 and given six months in prison for each violation, which she would serve consecutively, though they did dismiss the attempt to elude charge.

Reading all this, you might be thinking, "How stupid could this woman be?" But here's the thing: she wasn't. You could call her a lot of things—troubled, insecure, addicted, an opportunist, a habitual offender—but Ellen Ducharme was *far* from stupid. Instead of seeing that and intervening in some meaningful way, the justice system appeared to be popping out penalties without much thought, like a machine doling out gum balls. I can't be sure if there was ever any significant attempt to set her on the straight and narrow. Did the system abandon her, or was she just inherently willful? Both may be true.

An early booking photograph of Ellen Ducharme. *WCAX-TV.*

In 1992, she was popped for felony theft at a downtown department store, Steinbachs. The woman with one of the most prolific shoplifting histories I've ever seen was sentenced to six months to three years in prison, most of it suspended, and placed on probation.

In May 1990, Ellen had a son with her boyfriend Steave Castleman. It didn't temper her behavior.

A little more than three years later, in October 1993, Ellen was charged with conspiracy to distribute marijuana to prison inmates, a scheme that involved Castleman, a prison cook; Lloyd Touchette, one of the guards; Robert Payne; and her own father, Ron Lamphere.

According to official documents, Ducharme paid Payne to carry contraband to Castleman, who was serving time in the facility. Castleman sold the drugs on the inside, and because inmates were allowed to have no more than sixty dollars at any given time, his profits were given to the cook, who would send the money to Ellen's father in Burlington, who would then turn it over to Ellen. The cook and guard were both suspended. (I had a laugh when I read in the *Burlington Free Press* that Corrections Commissioner John Gorczyk had not decided whether Payne, the guard who was implicated, would be paid a salary during his suspension.)

Steave Castleman was given three years in prison for his part in the conspiracy, but Ellen's case was dismissed by the state. It would appear that keeping her on the outside was more valuable to the authorities than their need to teach her a lesson.

In the late '90s, I lost track of Ellen. The people I knew who knew her better than I did were no longer traveling in her circles. Then in 2004, Ligia Collins went missing.

Ligia Collins grew up in South Burlington, Vermont. Two years before her disappearance, the mother of two had completed a degree program in liberal arts at the Community College of Vermont. Her family said she was bright and outgoing and that she loved drawing and playing the saxophone.

On July 4, Collins left her home at 195 St. Paul Street and didn't return. The next day, her boyfriend Ramon Ryan contacted police, telling them she had gone to Ellen's house at midnight but never returned. The next day, police began a search for her using cadaver sniffing dogs, divers who searched the Winooski River and even helicopters. Her case brought to mind another missing person case: that of Brianna Maitland of Sheldon, Vermont, who had disappeared earlier in the year. Publicly, the police did not

Ligia Collins. *From the South Burlington High School Sentry.*

rule out the possibility of a connection, but following up on Ryan's report, they had already tried to contact Ellen, who called the station, leaving them a voicemail. As the situation unraveled, officers would meet with her seven times.

On Monday, July 12, while police were still tracking down leads and likely suspects, one of them, fifty-two-year-old Moses "Moey" Robar, shot himself in the parking lot of a roofing company on Briggs Street in Burlington's south end. The shooting occurred in broad daylight, and in no time, the street and lot were filled with police in tactical gear and neighbors wondering what the hubbub was.

Full disclosure: Robar was my cousin.

It's hard, even now, for me to grasp that someone I remember as a young marine returning from Vietnam, who presented me a gift shop lollypop the size of my head, is the same guy who shot himself because he was tangled up in a web of drug deals and murder. Life is full of surprises—not all of them pleasant.

The next day, another suspect was made public. Ellen, shackled and handcuffed, appeared in Vermont District Court, picked up on an unrelated probation violation. Now thirty-eight, she looked far different than I remembered. The intervening years had not treated her kindly. With Robar, her boyfriend, in the hospital post-surgery for severe head trauma, Ellen, now a mother of three, was held without bail and placed on suicide watch. The *Burlington Free Press* made sure to mention her sixty-four criminal charges since 1982. Robar had eleven, including a domestic violence charge for

Moses Robar, an accessory to the murder of Ligia Collins. *WCAX-TV.*

punching Ellen in the face the previous month. She'd been granted a restraining order against him shortly before Collins disappeared. During questioning, Ellen acknowledged she'd been using cocaine regularly for the past several months and had purchased it twice the night of July 4. Police, with two suspects but no corpse, felt all but certain Ligia Collins was dead.

Two days later, Moses Robar died from his self-inflicted gunshot wound. Previously, police had impounded his 1991 Chevy pickup. The truck, with its rusted wheel wells, had seen better days. The inside was littered with clothing and smelled of cigarettes. A brochure for people who had lost their licenses due to DUI infractions was found on the back seat. Police were asking anyone who had seen the vehicle between late July 5 and early July 6 to come forward.

On Saturday, July 31, around 6:30 p.m., nearly a month after she went missing, Ligia Collins's body was found in a wooded location in Ripton, Vermont. Her stepfather, Bruce Jean, was at a nearby command post when the body was discovered. Collins's family was devastated but still grateful she was found. Her mother, Louanne Collins, was quoted as saying, "It gives us closure. Under the circumstances, it can't get any better than this."

On August 3, came the fascinating news that a convicted axe murderer was the third suspect in the Collins murder. In 1987, Timothy Crews had killed a teenager, Craig Jackman of Essex, in the town of Westford and pleaded no contest to a charge of second-degree murder. Picked up on July 13 for violating the conditions of his release, he was cooling his heels, waiting for prosecutors to go over the finer points of the evidence.

More than a week later, details of the murder were fleshed out for a curious public. Police revealed Ligia Collins's death was the result of a drug deal gone wrong.

Ellen, after first claiming Robar had killed Collins, had confessed. She said that Collins, carrying drugs she intended to sell, had shown up at her home at 221 North Avenue (the location of that long-ago baby shower), armed with a .45-caliber handgun that belonged to Robar that had disappeared weeks earlier. The two argued, and Ellen, already high on crack, picked up a baseball bat. As Collins walked away, Ellen hit her in the back of the head. Collins fought back, and in a rage, Ellen beat her to death. She then opened the door to the basement and shoved Collins's body downstairs.

When the visiting Crews saw Collins's body, he suggested Ellen clean the house and then went with Robar to dispose of the corpse. They took it to the woods in Ripton, a place Robar, an avid hunter, was familiar with. Interestingly, during her interview, Ellen made clear to police that in spite of everything that had gone down, her boyfriend hadn't wanted her to use drugs and just wanted a normal life. This jibes with what Frank Ducharme, the brother of Ellen's first husband, Charlie, told the *Burlington Free Press*. He said when he'd last talked to Robar, he'd spoken of wanting to change his life.

In court, Ellen's lawyer, Bob Katims, pleaded not guilty on her behalf, and Judge James Crucitti ordered her to be held without bail, facing thirty-five years to life in prison.

Crews, who originally admitted his part in the killing during phone conversations with police, had pleaded not guilty but ultimately changed his plea. In March 2005, he pleaded guilty to being an accessory after the fact in exchange for dismissal of a habitual offender charge that could have meant life in prison. The accessory charge was punishable by up to seven years in prison. Crews had cooperated with the investigation and had helped police find Ligia's body by drawing a map. The deal made sense.

During a hearing in January 2006, Ellen's confession in the death of Ligia Collins was deemed inadmissible in court, because investigators, threatening her with the death penalty, had questioned her without an attorney present. In his ruling, the judge wrote, "Since Vermont is not a death penalty state, citizens are not inured to the suggested application of the death penalty. It is time to recognize the threat for what it is, especially in Vermont."

On July 26, 2006, Ellen accepted a deal, pleading guilty in exchange for a reduction in her charge from first- to second-degree murder. With the change in plea, she could argue for a prison term as short as four years. The cat being out of the bag regarding police threatening the death penalty in order to obtain her confession, prosecutors knew they'd have trouble proving the murder was premeditated. Still, they could ask the court to give Ellen a sentence of twenty-five years in prison, five more than the typical maximum under state law.

On November 28, 2006, Ellen went to court expecting to be sentenced for Collins's murder, but Judge Michael Kupersmith, citing the gap in expectations between the prosecution and the defense in what her sentence might be, said extra time was needed to reach a conclusion, "We'll try to get it in before the holidays."

On Tuesday, December 12, Kupersmith was ready.

Before her sentencing, Ellen, citing a migraine, asked her lawyer to read a statement, which was brief: "It was never my intention to take another's life. I can only deeply regret what I have done and offer an apology."

Ellen Ducharme had at last committed a crime that would result in long-term jail time. She was sentenced to twenty-five years to life in prison for the murder of Ligia Collins.

18

A BEAUTIFUL GIRL

As this book indicates, Burlington's been no stranger to homicide. Still, in 2006, we felt relatively safe from the kinds of cold-blooded crimes seen in major cities. But that was before a bright young woman brimming with potential, a twenty-one-year-old named Michelle Gardner-Quinn, was raped and slain by a stranger she'd turned to in a time of need.

Michelle Gardner-Quinn, born on January 28, 1985, in Washington, D.C., was an undergraduate at the University of Vermont. She had previously been enrolled at Goucher College in Baltimore, Maryland, where she'd split her time between on-campus studies and trips to Costa Rica, South Africa and Brazil. Intensely interested in our world and its environment, Michelle had recently transferred to UVM because it allowed her to design a combined environmental studies and Latin American studies major. The fact that she enjoyed hiking and was an avid snow boarder who had already made friends in Vermont was the icing on the cake.

It would come as no surprise to anyone meeting Michelle that the captivating girl with the hazel eyes had arrived in Burlington with a ready-made fan base. Called light-hearted but wise with a "funky" sense of humor, she was full of energy with no shortage of interests. From activism to photography, to jumping cliffs on her bike, she was always on the move.

It appeared Michelle learned best by doing. Her friend Georgeanne Usova, in an interview for *Cosmopolitan* magazine's feature story "Murder of a Beautiful Girl," said, "I was studying political theory, writing papers

UVM student Michelle
Gardner Quinn. *WCAX-TV.*

about the plight of Costa Rican plantation workers. She [Michelle] went there and lived with them in extreme poverty, then came home to tell about it."

The weekend of October 6–8, 2006, was a busy one for the UVM, the university on the hill, and for businesses across the Burlington area. It was alumni and parents weekend, an annual event that occurs during a period when the downtown area is already overflowing with foliage season visitors. Michelle's parents, John-Charles Quinn and Diane Gardner, were visiting from their home in Arlington, Virginia, and the three arranged to spend time together on Saturday. Michelle already had Friday night plans; a friend was turning twenty-one and a group of students were going to be celebrating the occasion with dinner and a bit of youthful barhopping.

She met her friends downtown, and eventually, Friday night turned into Saturday morning. Michelle was the first to leave the group. She was supposed to meet a friend near the Ski Rack at the corner of Main and Pine Streets, but they didn't connect. According to her friend Tommy Lang, who spoke with her by phone, she was last known to be walking up Main Street toward campus at 2:15 a.m., with some "random guy" who'd let her use his cellphone because her phone's battery had died. "She sounded completely fine and normal and exactly the way she did when she left us," he said. "There wasn't anything that made me worry or made me suspicious that anything was going on."

But the next day, as friends tried to reach Michelle, their messages went unanswered. One friend, Ian Wilson, had spoken with her on Friday. When he tried to reach her on Saturday, he got no response, and, finally worried, he began leaving long messages asking her to *please* call him back.

Michelle's parents, John-Charles and Diane, were also anxious to hear from their daughter. When she failed to join them as previously arranged, they went to her residence hall, but she wasn't there. Their concern loomed larger as the hours passed. Being out of touch like this was unlike her. Michelle could be spontaneous, but she wasn't irresponsible. Knowing there had to be a reason she wasn't answering their calls, they filed a missing person report with the local police.

I recall 2006 as the year Facebook opened its membership beyond students to anyone over the age of thirteen, and I was still figuring out how the tool might work for me. But Michelle's friends *were* students, already social media savvy. They posted the following message.

> *PLEASE HELP!!! Our friend Michelle Gardner-Quinn has been certified as missing….Michelle is a white female, 5 feet 8 inches, 135 pounds, shoulder-length brown hair. She was wearing a gray peacoat with toggle clasps, and her nose is pierced.*
>
> *She was last seen on Friday night/Saturday morning at a bar in downtown Burlington, Vermont and last spoken to on a cell phone….If you are afraid to call police but you know something PLEASE STILL HELP US. Let me know any information at all.*

Students began making posters and distributing fliers. Soon, "MISSING" posters were plastered all over the downtown area and the campus on the hill.

At a press conference on October 10, her parents pleaded for the public's help. Her mother said, "I think she's a fighter. I think she's resourceful….We pray that she's alive."

Reports of possible suspects began swirling through the community. The school's student newspaper, the *Vermont Cynic*, reported that, according to police, the man Michelle had been walking with up Main Street, who was not believed to be a student, was not a suspect. Additional information stated the police were searching for "a white male in his 20s driving a Subaru-type hatchback" who was seen trying to coax another woman into his car a short time before Michelle's disappearance.

Time is always a critical factor in missing persons cases. The longer Michelle was missing, the more people worried. Investigators and canine teams were working around the clock, and by October 11, Burlington's chief of police Thomas Tremblay announced teams would be expanding search grids, with the FBI and the national guard joining in to assist. Police asked anyone in the general public who might also be assisting in the search not to touch any evidence they might find but to immediately call the department.

On the UVM campus and across the city, the mood was tense. People who might normally feel perfectly safe walking alone changed their habits. Authorities urged citizens to walk in groups or pairs, to stay in well-lit areas away from dense shrubbery and to be aware of their surroundings. They also encouraged people to stay away from trouble by trusting their instincts.

Days went by with little news or hope. Police did not comment on how many search warrants were issued. They continued to follow leads and eliminate suspects.

On October 12, police still hadn't found Michelle and were operating on the assumption that she had been abducted but was still alive. A plea went out to the public for residents to search their yards for a list of items Michelle may have been wearing or had on her person the night she disappeared: earrings, a wood-bead bracelet and her university ID card.

On October 13, contrary to some previous reports, the *Burlington Free Press* revealed that the man who had offered Michelle Gardner Quinn his cellphone the night she disappeared had become "a significant focus" of the investigation. The police weren't any closer to making an arrest or finding the missing girl, but it was another piece of the puzzle. One more "puzzle piece" surfaced thanks to the diligent work of a member of the Burlington Police Department, Detective Andrew Frisbie.

These days, people are accustomed to random surveillance, but in 2006 in downtown Burlington, technology like that was rare. BPD's Detective Andrew Frisbie canvassed businesses in search of any building with security cameras and discovered that a store called Perrywinkle's Fine Jewelry, a relatively new addition to the downtown, had cameras that pointed toward the sidewalk outside its Main Street location. Examining the security footage,

Perrywinkles Jewelry, Main Street. *Roger Lewis.*

detectives could see Michelle Gardner-Quinn and a man police could not yet identify strolling a few feet apart on the south side of Main Street, headed up the hill toward Edmunds Middle School.

On the heels of this new evidence came the news that Michelle's family, friends and the community had been dreading. At 1:00 p.m. on October 13, the search for Michelle Gardner-Quinn ended. Her partially naked body had been discovered by a hiker in a previously unexamined area at the lip of Huntington Gorge in Richmond, Vermont.

That afternoon, Chief Tremblay, in an emotional press conference, advised the public that Michelle had been found and offered another shocking revelation: based on the evidence, he was prepared to identify her killer as thirty-six-year-old Brian Rooney, an unemployed construction worker who was being held on prior charges. The chief promised to give the public more information as soon as it was available and asked everyone to keep Michelle's family in their thoughts and prayers.

Brian Rooney, the man with the cellphone, was the last person to see Michelle alive, and police, armed with enough circumstantial evidence, had been granted multiple search warrants that included Rooney's car and places he was living or had stayed and a request for full-body photographs, photographs that revealed fresh scratch marks, still red and beginning to scar over, on his back and hands. Much later, an autopsy would reveal abrasions and contusions on Michelle's right hand. It was proof the young woman had fought back.

Michelle had suffered two wounds to her head, an indication of blunt-force trauma, and marks on her neck indicted strangulation. She had been sexually assaulted.

That Friday night, the UVM campus was dotted with points of candlelight, as several hundred people, Michelle's fellow students, held memorials for her. They sat in circles or stood huddled together, cellphones silenced. Some were crying.

In a *Burlington Free Press* story written by reporter Sam Hemingway, published the day Michelle's body was discovered, Rooney's older brother Rikki revealed Rooney's childhood had been what one might call pillar to post. The father of the family's three oldest children had run off, leaving them vulnerable. They moved houses frequently. Rikki called it "kind of funny" that his brother had been arrested on outstanding charges for crimes that occurred years before. He also claimed Brian Rooney, who was the father of three daughters, was a "devoted family man." "You'll never find a better parent," Rikki Rooney said. "He lives for his kids."

But other news accounts of Brian Rooney's past painted a darker picture. In an affidavit filed in Vermont District Court in St. Johnsbury, Vermont, Rooney was accused of molestation in both 1996 and 1998; the victim was twelve and fourteen years old at the time of the assaults. It was alleged that he also made advances toward her sister. Over the course of the proceedings, it was revealed Rooney had used chemical-soaked rags and other substances to render his victims unconscious and unable to resist his sexual advances. He was charged with sexual assault and lewd and lascivious conduct. Additionally, Rooney had a history of making death threats to women who'd broken off their relationships with him. Burlington Police lieutenants Tim Charland and Emmet Helrich spoke with one, who was the mother of one of Brian Rooney's children. She told them she was afraid of Rooney, who once, upon seeing her chatting with a male coworker, threatened to cut off all her hair. She told the officers he'd never wanted her to get pregnant and had threatened that if she did, he would shoot her.

While Rooney was protesting his innocence, there were mounting clues that he wasn't on the up and up. He repeatedly changed his story while being interviewed. A specially trained dog had strongly reacted to Michelle's scent in his vehicle, even though he told police she was never inside. In one sworn account, he told authorities, "If I did it, I deserve to die." In a statement to Corporal Ray Nails of the BPD, he said he didn't remember much of what he

had done the night of Michelle's disappearance, citing the fact that he was "extremely drunk." But this didn't stop him from driving his own car home that night. Rooney had already picked up a charge of DWI, or "driving while intoxicated," in February 2000, for which he pleaded guilty and was fined $300.

A court-ordered DNA test that he submitted to on October 19 absolutely linked him to the crime. Marcia LaFountain, a forensic scientist who worked on Michelle's case, testified that the probability of randomly selecting an unrelated individual in the general population with the combination of DNA types found in the sample taken from Michelle's body was roughly 1 in 240 quadrillion. Brian Rooney was arraigned on

Brian Rooney. *WCAX-TV.*

charges of aggravated murder while perpetrating

a sexual assault. He would, if convicted, receive a sentence of life in prison without parole. His defense attorney David Sleigh entered a plea of not guilty.

Post arraignment, Sleigh stated, "We'd like to remind people that Brian is presumed innocent, and he's in fact innocent.…We intend to test the strength of the state's case in a court of law."

Michelle's friends and family and an eager public awaited news of the trial as Sleigh and Prosecutor Rosemary Gretkowski for the state prepared to make their case.

It was important to Sleigh to get the trial out of Chittenden County. He filed a motion to get it moved to another court, claiming pretrial publicity—including an editorial piece in which Rooney was described by an FBI agent as "evil"—would make it impossible to provide his client with an unbiased jury draw. He also pointed to an op-ed about the case in the weekly newspaper *Seven Days*, written by "an anonymous cop," and the fact the *Burlington Free Press* had published ninety-four stories that referenced the case as evidence of his theory. Prosecutor Gretkowski opposed the move, saying publicity alone didn't prove prejudice, but once all was said and done, Sleigh's request won out.

On May 13, 2008, jury selection for the trial began. Vermont is a small state, and even with a change of venue, it would have been unrealistic to think potential jurors were completely ignorant of the terrible events that occurred in Burlington during the fall of 2006. Judge Michael Kupersmith cautioned potential jurors they would have to make their decision based solely on the evidence they heard in the trial, saying, "As twenty-first-century adults, you know that what the media presents to us is not necessarily accurate."

Still, it was a crime most people took personally. During jury selection, David Sleigh questioned a man who was the coach of a women's cross-country team. The would-be juror explained to the court that, because of his coaching, he was protective of women in their twenties. It prompted Sleigh to ask if the man thought he could vote to acquit, since Michelle had been twenty-one, if there was evidence to support Rooney's innocence. The man answered, "I'd like to say, with my character, yes. But I'm not sure."

Once selected, the jury was inundated with evidence. They saw police reports, cellphone records and lab tests. They saw the freeze-frame video captured by the cameras at Perrywinkle's Fine Jewelry. In a darkened courtroom, they saw forty minutes' worth of autopsy photographs. There were expert witnesses, DNA findings and even Michelle's torn peacoat, her favorite coat, the one she'd been wearing the night she was murdered, with its ripped seam and missing toggle button. They heard the moving testimony of Michelle's friends and family.

The jury began their deliberations on May 22, just before 11:30 a.m. After being sequestered for more than six hours, they found Brian Rooney guilty of aggravated murder. After the verdict was delivered, Michelle's mother Diane said, "Justice works once in a while. Twenty months is a long time."

Brian Rooney was sentenced to life in prison without the possibility of parole. In the ensuing years, there was a smattering of appeals and a demand for a retrial but to no avail. He is currently serving his sentence at the Lee Adjustment Center in Beattyville, Kentucky.

19

A PROMISE OF SILENCE

Only a few months after I said goodbye to my job at a local TV station to write books and lead tours full time, a news story appeared on the air and online that was nearly inescapable. On Wednesday, June 8, 2011, an Essex, Vermont couple, William and Lorraine Currier, left their respective jobs for the day and were never seen again. When Lorraine, who worked in patient financial services at Fletcher Allen Healthcare, failed to show up at work Thursday morning and didn't call in, it was cause for concern among her coworkers. As the morning went by, their worrying escalated. It just wasn't like Lorraine, who rarely took a day off anyway to be absent without notice. They decided to call her husband at the University of Vermont. When officials there told them Bill, who worked at UVM as an animal technician, was also uncharacteristically absent without word, they feared something was terribly wrong.

It was William Currier's sister Diana Smith who eventually called the police, and officers went to the couple's home at 8 Colbert Street to do a welfare check. The tidy, one-level house, known to neighbors for its festive outdoor decorations during the holidays, was empty. Essex police, surveying the scene, had reason to believe there had been foul play. Not only were the Curriers gone, but their dark green Saturn sedan was missing from the home as well. A smashed window in an interior door and other clues were a giveaway that the couple had not left their house voluntarily. Both the Curriers took prescription medication that had been left behind, along with their Lorraine's purse and her husband's wallet. It was an unsettling state of

The Colbert Street home of Bill and Lorraine Currier. *Roger Lewis.*

affairs for residents in what was normally a peaceful, quiet neighborhood. Neighbors, along with the Curriers' friends, family and coworkers waited anxiously for any news. The couple's bank accounts and phone records were checked. Neither had been used.

Bill and Lorraine Currier were married in 1985 and lived together in an apartment in the city of Winooski while looking for their dream home. They found it in 2003, nestled in a family neighborhood just five minutes from the Champlain Valley Exposition. They'd each worked in their respective jobs for more than twenty years. Friends said Bill, who enlisted in the army right after high school, was filled with curiosity about everything from space exploration to politics. Lorraine, described as an outgoing person with many friends, enjoyed baking special treats for relatives. Family-oriented, she loved spending time at camp with her sisters and nieces. Both Lorraine and Bill took on the task of documenting their family's history and events—Lorraine with an ever-present video camera and Bill with photograph albums and genealogical research. Though the couple had no children of their own, they were close to their nieces and nephews, inviting them to the movies and over to their house on weekends. Summers were special times for them, with free time spent in their garden or relaxing by the pool. Now, with summer stretching out ahead of them, Bill, fifty, and Lorraine, fifty-five, were nowhere to be found.

By June 17, William Currier's mother, Marilyn Chates, was given limited guardianship in order to protect the missing couple's assets, and a $10,000 reward was offered by the family for information leading to the couple's whereabouts. Essex Police, collaborating with the FBI, eventually found the Curriers' car but not the Curriers. Later, it was deduced by investigators who compared mileage numbers from a past service record with the known trips the Curriers' car typically made that there was a distance of about forty miles that was unaccounted for. A sighting by an unidentified witness resulted in a police sketch of man who had been seen driving the vehicle, and police were looking for a gun that had recently been purchased by the Curriers and was kept by Lorraine under her mattress.

By June 22, two emotional weeks had passed since the Curriers had gone missing, and still, there was no word. Police could only let the public know there was no information to report and that they were still looking for leads. They assured anyone who came forward that their tips would be handled in a confidential manner.

Local media, eager for background information on the case, were disturbed to be denied information that was being kept confidential by investigators. The *Burlington Free Press* filed an appeal to access the search warrants related to the case, but the Vermont Supreme Court ruled that the materials would remain sealed. In early July, the *Burlington Free Press* wrote the justices, saying the paper was aware there were times that, to preserve the integrity of an investigation, materials should be sealed, but it believed the government should have to provide detailed reasons why a particular piece of information was so critical to the case that it must be.

A month after the couple's disappearance, there was still no word. Police had pored over the Curriers' computer records and had viewed surveillance video from at least twenty-five businesses in and around Essex. Acting Essex Chief of Police Brad LaRose made it clear that foul play was suspected. Court records requested by the *Burlington Free Press* were still sealed. On July 20, it was learned that the Essex Select Board had approved the use of up to $15,000 for DNA testing in the case. Chief LaRose declined to say exactly who or what the testing was for. He also confirmed that cadaver sniffing dogs from the Massachusetts State Police had been brought in to assist in the search. Also in July, LaRose finally revealed publicly what some of the mystery search warrants and subpoenas were for. They were obtained to

Essex murder victims Bill and Lorraine Currier. *WCAX-TV.*

secure bank and phone records and to search the Curriers' house, their car and a dumpster next to where the car had been found.

On August 5, police broadened their search, with teams operating on foot fanned out about a hundred yards on either side of the road in rural parts of Essex, places a body might be found or where evidence might land after being thrown from a car window. These ground searches would continue until late October.

Fast-forward to February 2012 and long-awaited news. It was revealed that police had gotten a court order to obtain three sets of fingerprints from an unnamed suspect; however, the information was followed by another long period of quiet.

Then, on April 12, 2012, passersby could not help but notice a significant amount of activity at a demolished home at 32 Upper Main Street in Essex, near Lang Farm. Chief LaRose told reporters he wasn't ready to make any statements about what the workers, who were dressed in Hazmat suits, or the dogs present at the location were looking for, but a lead investigator acknowledged it was related to the Currier case. The search moved to a landfill in Coventry owned by Casella Waste Management, a site that was the repository for the construction debris from the house on Upper Main Street. With the federal agents taking a lead role, 178 FBI agents and members of the Essex Police and the Vermont State Police pored over more than ten thousand pounds of trash during a search that cost $1 million.

But the dig ended with no word on what—if anything—had been found.

There was a reason for the silence. The FBI had a suspect, and during interviews, they promised not to reveal his identity in exchange for his cooperation. The deal worked until July 2012, when Jennifer Reading, a reporter working at WCAX, named the Curriers' killer based on an anonymous tip. Though other news entities in the area kept a lid on the information, word spread to the suspect, who was being held in Alaska. His word was good. There were no more details forthcoming.

In September, as reported by the *Burlington Free Press*, the Curriers' family requested death certificates be issued for the pair, and law enforcement disclosed they had received information the previous April that the Curriers had been forcibly removed from their home and taken to the empty house on Upper Main Street, where they had been killed by their abductor. The investigation at the house earlier in the year indicated human remains had been present at the site, but no bodies were found. Bill and Lorraine were presumed dead, and a judge ordered the medical examiner to issue the certificates. It wasn't until December 2012 that Vermonters finally heard the name of their killer: Israel Keyes.

Israel Keyes was born on January 7, 1978, the second oldest of ten children to John and Heidi Keyes. From his earliest years in Cove, Utah, the place of his birth, his was a nontraditional upbringing. His parents, followers of the Church of Jesus Christ of Latter-day Saints, raised their brood off the grid, without modern conveniences. At one point, the family shared a one-room cabin in the woods with no heat, running water or electricity. Some of the kids slept in a tent.

When Keyes was five, John and Heidi relocated with their children to Colville, Washington. Opposed to government interference and relying heavily on faith, they homeschooled their children and didn't believe in modern medicine. It was there that they decided to leave the Mormon faith and began attending a fundamentalist Christian church that preached white supremacy. As a teen, Keyes's psychopathic tendencies threw him into the company of friends who were like-minded and up to no good. It was in Coleville that he met and befriended Chevie Kehoe, a murderer and member of the Aryan Peoples' Republic who, as I write this, is serving three consecutive life sentences for the kidnapping, torture and murder of an entire Arkansas family.

Keyes and his siblings, practicing independence while contributing to the family's bottom line, did odd jobs for cash. For recreation, Keyes broke into homes and started fires in the woods. He carried a pistol everywhere he went. With a friend, he burglarized houses. Always an avid hunter, he began killing and torturing pets.

John and Heidi, who seemed to always be looking for their religion, moved the family to a Quaker community in Smyrna, Maine, where they ran a maple sugaring operation. After declaring himself an atheist, Keyes was kicked out of the house but remained close to his mother.

In the late '90s he committed his first kidnapping, abduction and rape of a teenage hiker, whom he later released. Not long after, at the age of twenty, he joined the army and seemed to do well, despite receiving a charge of driving while intoxicated during his period of enlistment. Former army friends said he was a quiet person who kept to himself. He spent his weekends drinking heavily, his alcohol of choice being Wild Turkey bourbon. Keyes was honorably discharged and even received an achievement medal for "meritorious service while assigned as a gunner and assistant gunner from the second of December 1998 to the eighth of July, 2001 in the Alpha Company 60mm mortar section."

Unlike serial killer Ted Bundy, Keyes didn't have a "type"; he just preyed on victims who happened to show up where he was. He liked remote places, like parks, cemeteries and campgrounds, where there was no one around; therefore, there were no witnesses. He studied other serial killers so he could hone his "craft," and Ted Bundy was his hero. Maybe you've seen pictures of Ted Bundy's "murder kit." Keyes had many. He would travel to various locations and bury the covered buckets that contained his tools of his trade: guns, ammunition, plastic sheets and Drano. Eventually, he'd go back to the location and pick a victim at random. Before he killed Bill and Lorraine Currier in Essex, he was in Chicago. Before that, he was in Alaska. Traveling to different locales to kill, he always paid in cash and took the battery out of his cellphone so he couldn't be tracked. It's been speculated he went so far as to have lap-band surgery to decrease his need for food while capturing and killing his victims.

In 2000, Keyes became involved with a woman who lived on the Makah Reservation in Washington. Their daughter was born the next year. During an interview while in custody, Keyes mentioned he wanted his child to have a normal life, "without all this hanging over her head."

Though Bill and Lorraine Currier were his first confirmed victims, Keyes told the FBI he actually began his killing spree in 2001. He said his one rule through the years was that he would never harm children or anyone who had a child, because he had a daughter of his own. The FBI, believing he'd killed adolescents, were skeptical of this claim.

On February 1, 2002, Keyes planned his last kill, kidnapping a barista named Samantha Koenig from a coffee shop called Common Grounds in Anchorage, Alaska. Samantha was working alone, and seeing the opportunity, Keyes abducted, raped and imprisoned her before he killed her the following day. He stole her debit card and then went on vacation. Returning days later to Anchorage and the shed where he'd hidden Samantha's body, he posed her body as though she was alive and demanded a ransom from her family, which was to be deposited into her bank account. He spent the next month traveling through Arizona, New Mexico and Texas, disguising himself while using ATMs to take money out of the dead woman's account. On March 13, police in Lufkin, Texas, picked Keyes up for a speeding violation. On him, he had Samantha's stolen debit card and phone.

Authorities, interested in wheedling every bit of information from Keyes they could, fancied up their sit-downs with him, bringing in coffee and treats. He was not an easy prisoner. In the spring of 2012, he tried to run from a courtroom and was tackled and tasered by U.S. marshals. He was also disciplined for MacGyvering a device to open his handcuffs. Every time he left his cell, the wily killer had to be escorted by not one but two guards.

Originally housed in the mental health unit of the prison, he was eventually no longer considered a suicide risk and moved to Bravo Module, a maximum-security unit for long-term prisoners.

While he was incarcerated, investigators learned a lot about why he picked the Curriers. One reason was the layout of their house. Keyes told the FBI he chose the home because the couple seemed to have no kids and no dog. Their house had an attached garage, and the style of the house helped him figure out the likely location of Bill and Lorraine's bedroom. Upon cutting the phone line, he discovered there was no security system. He then removed a fan from an exterior window to access the garage and smashed a window inside with a crowbar to gain entrance to the house. The couple, who had arrived home from work by 7:00 p.m. were likely preparing for bed when he broke into their home. Police later found that Bill had already laid out his clothes for work the next day. Keyes bound Bill and Lorraine with zip ties and took them in their car to the house on Upper Main Street, a place he'd already

A booking photograph of serial killer Israel Keyes. *FBI file.*

scoped out. He left Lorraine in the car while he took Bill to the basement of the structure and tied him to a stool. Going back for Lorraine, he found she'd managed to escape. He tackled her and brought her inside the house. Then he shot Bill and, afterward, sexually assaulted and strangled Lorraine. He wrapped their bodies in garbage bags and concealed them with debris he'd collected in the basement. He threw the murder weapon he'd brought from Alaska and the gun he'd taken from the Currier home into a reservoir in New York. Based on information provided by Keyes, the weapons were recovered by FBI dive teams.

According to an interview session recorded on November 29, 2012, Keyes took exception to the release of information about his crimes that he felt ran contrary to the "deal" he'd made with the FBI. The Vermont case was mentioned. New leaks were frustrating him. Despite being a cold-blooded killer, the man described as a "doting father" was concerned that the details of what he'd done and the inevitable rumors would harm his child. He decided he no longer had much to gain by talking.

On December 1, 2012, Keyes was seen moving about his cell in Bravo Module and settling into bed a little after 10:00 p.m. As he normally did, he covered his entire body and face with a blanket. It's thought, based on movement in Keyes's cell as seen on surveillance video, that at around 10:24 p.m., using a makeshift noose that he wrapped around his neck and a razor that had mistakenly been issued to him, Keyes took his own life. Despite sixteen checks of the cellblock during his shift, the guard on duty, Loren Jacobsen, did not see the blood pooling on the floor of Keyes's cell. The killer's dead body was discovered by a day-shift officer at 6:00 a.m.

20

UNSOLVED

Marsha Lamonda

Twenty-five-year-old Marsha Lamonda was reported missing by her father on July 6, 1977. Lamonda, a 1969 graduate of South Burlington High School, suffered the degenerative brain disease Huntington's chorea, but friends described her as reasonably happy despite her illness. She'd last been seen June 30, exiting a North Street Bar in Burlington. Lamonda, who previously worked for a credit reporting company, was unemployed at the time of her disappearance. Though mystery still shrouds her death, her remains were found ten years later off Bean Road in Charlotte, Vermont. Her skull was found by a neighbor of the property who was out for a walk. Authorities were alerted, and searches were conducted by state police mobile crime scene personnel. By the time Lamonda's body was found, her parents were both deceased. Her ex-husband, Kenneth Lamonda, commented that before her disappearance, she was "hanging with a bad crowd on North Street."

John McGrath

On October 10, 1974, the body of bar and restaurant manager John McGrath was found inside the Green Mountain Lunch in Winooski.

Neighbors heard shots shortly after McGrath was dropped off at the restaurant by his son, sometime between 7:00 and 7:30 a.m. A man named George Ladabouche entered the business to investigate and found McGrath, a veteran of World War II, lying on the floor next to the pool table, dead from a gunshot wound. The victim's wallet was missing, but the money in the till was untouched. Despite an intense search that included over a dozen interviews and numerous anonymous tips, the murder remains unsolved.

WENDELL JOHN EMSLIE

Wendell John Emslie, described as a friendly, honest and punctual person, was reported missing by his wife on March 23, 1977, when he did not return home as expected. At the time of his disappearance, the sixty-three-year-old Shelburne man, who had retired from a job at the Beneficial Finance Co., was working as a courier and salesman-collector for Lippa's Jewelers in downtown Burlington.

Emslie's car was found in the parking lot of Burlington's Ethan Allen Shopping Center on North Avenue. An eventual investigation into the victim's driving habits and a check of the car's odometer indicated it had been driven an additional fifty miles. Wendell's body was eventually found on an island in the Winooski River, near the Bolton-Duxbury town line. He'd been killed with a small-caliber gun.

The money he would have had on his person at the time was missing, but the jewelry items he'd been transporting were locked inside his yellow Pinto with the keys left inside the vehicle.

WILFRED KING III

Thirty-seven-year-old Wilfred "Butch" King III was reported missing from his home on Jericho Road in Essex on October 24, 1980. At the time of his disappearance, the five-foot-four-inch-tall King was wearing a silver belt buckle with a 1776–1976 design and an inexpensive wristwatch.

The day after the report was issued, bloodstained metal crutches belonging to King, who'd been injured in a car accident a few years before, were found by two hunters, who turned them over to Colchester Police.

Weeks later, King's burned-out blue and white 1979 Chevy Blazer was found in the Oak Hill gravel pit in Williston. A search of the area resulted in no leads.

Despite numerous police interviews and anonymous tips, King's body was never recovered.

Lloyd "Pat" Fitzgerald

Lloyd "Pat" Fitzgerald, a twenty-seven-year-old electrician who made his home on Gazo Avenue in Burlington, was last seen on October 2, 1972.

The employee of the Burlington Electric Department, who was doing a private job for Dr. Paul Levi on Van Patten Parkway, left the Levi residence at about 9:30 p.m. His 1972 Chevy Vega station wagon was found the following day, parked west of North Avenue in the area of Lakewood Estates. His wife, Maureen, said she could think of no reason the father of three small children, ages two, three and five, would have left home with no word.

Bloodhounds following Fitzgerald's scent led searchers from his car through a wooded area and to a dirt road, where they lost the trail. His body was found in a cornfield near the Ethan Allen homestead five months later. His feet were bound. He had apparently been dragged to the location. The cause of his death was determined to be a gunshot wound. His death was ruled a homicide by the chief medical examiner.

"Big Bobbie" Fuller

The body of twenty-six-year-old unemployed waitress "Big Bobbie" Fuller was discovered on October 5, 1963, by two children who saw her lifeless form lying on a rock ledge beneath the Winooski Bridge. An autopsy revealed Bobbie, an excellent swimmer, had drowned. Her time of death was recorded as 6:00 a.m. The rock ledge where her body been found had not been submerged at that time.

Authorities only flirted with a ruling of foul play, since many questions surrounding her death remained unanswered. Though she'd previously mentioned her intention of jumping off the bridge, it was determined Bobbie did not fall, nor did she jump the twenty-nine-foot distance. Her blood alcohol level, .31, indicated she'd been very intoxicated, but the "tattooed woman," as she was called in local papers, sustained no internal injuries and had few bruises and only minor scratches when her body was recovered. Found next to her were her unbroken eyeglasses, her lower denture plate and an empty beer bottle—standing upright. The coroner Dr. Woodruff said, "The whole thing is awful peculiar. I don't think she even was on the bridge."

WILMA SCRIBNER

Wilma Scribner, forty-two, of Middlebury, Vermont, was reported missing on November 2, 1977, by her husband, Dana, after she didn't return home from shopping. When the body of the mother of eight, who worked as a night supervisor at Porter Medical Center, was found in in the Otter Creek in Weybridge in March 1979, the autopsy revealed she'd died by strangulation. Eight months later, her car, a dark green wood-paneled 1968 Ford LTD station wagon, license plate C-8037, was found in Otter Creek in an area upstream from where her body was located.

JAN RHEIN

The body of twenty-nine-year-old Jan Rhein was found on April 19, 1980, behind the old Forest Hills Store on West Canal Street in Winooski. It was discovered by a fisherman who was on his way to the Salmon Hole, and he hurried to alert authorities. Winooski Police Chief Roger A. Willard arrived on scene at 4:21 a.m. to determine Rhein was the victim of a gunshot wound. Rhein, who had prior convictions for drug use and had also previously been treated for self-inflicted gunshot wounds, had called police headquarters earlier in the week stating he had a problem. He did not disclose the problem, however, and, later in the conversation, said he would take care of it himself. Though it was deduced he may have been killed with his own gun, his death was determined to be the result of a homicide.

MARAM AND ROLAND HANEL

On September 20, 1984, the bodies of Maram and Roland Hanel of Jay, Vermont, were discovered at their residence by a neighbor. Known to rent out part of their chalet for extra income, the couple had no tenants at the time of the murder.

The pair, who were living off the interest from the sale of a Montreal plastics company, were described as a friendly and athletic couple who typically kept to themselves. Last seen alive on September 14 that year, they were found in separate rooms of the home and had each been shot numerous times.

MICHAEL DURENLEAU

Michael "Alky" Durenleau was attacked on July 12, 1985, after he and his wife, Rebecca, left an Essex Junction bar. The unknown assailant or assailants bludgeoned Durenleau, stabbing him twice in the heart during the attack. The murder was thought to be the result of a lovers' triangle, and Durenleau's wife was ultimately convicted of the crime. She was later acquitted, the decision overturned by the Vermont Supreme Court. The case is considered "unsolved."

KEITH DESTROMP

The body of Keith Destromp was discovered by a friend on May 30, 1989. It was found in a shed adjoining the former Pease Grain Elevator on Lake Street in Burlington, and his death was ruled a homicide by the chief medical examiner. Destromp, who grew up in the town of Underhill, was a veteran of the U.S. Marine Corps. The former construction laborer was also the father of two children, whose photographs were found in his wallet after his death.

Houseless at the time of his murder, Destromp was the victim of severe blunt trauma, the details of which police withheld, as they and the perpetrator were presumably the only ones to know the type of weapon used and the extent of Destromp's injuries.

Michael Gembarowski

On September 9, 1995, Milton Police were called to 58 McMullen Road in Milton, Vermont, to conduct a welfare check. After forcing entry into the residence, they discovered the body of Michael Gembarowski, the chief mechanic for the Bowl New England chain, lying on the kitchen floor. While it was initially believed Gembarowski died of natural causes, an autopsy revealed he was shot to death in his home, and his death was ruled a homicide.

21

FROM THE POLICE BLOTTER

THE APPLE DOESN'T FALL FAR

In December 1921, local police finally caught up with a man who'd been brazenly poaching poultry in Burlington. Hildred Jones, the son of the infamous Battery Street brawler May (Jones) Bee, was nabbed in the vicinity of Cherry and South Champlain Streets. Though all his chickens had apparently gone off to roost in the stewpots of his patrons, officers were confident they had enough evidence for an arrest.

Jones, who'd hit henhouses in neighborhoods all over the city—some of them twice—had ruffled quite a few feathers, as it was thought, based on his prolific thievery, that he was actually running an entire *ring* of chicken thieves.

Word on the street was that he charged twenty-five cents a pound, but police had a hard time confirming that number, since Jones's customers, feeling they'd gotten a good deal, weren't inclined to squawk.

A ST. ALBANS DIVERSION

You probably know that it's easier to buy potatoes than grow them, especially if you've got a yard like mine—boggy in spots and covered in shade. I've tried digging trenches, mulching, planting in raised beds and even using the

St. Albans residents were given permission to "let the dogs out." *Library of Congress Archives.*

old chicken wire potato tower trick, but the potatoes are always so small, it just isn't worth the effort.

Despite my ineptitude at raising a decent tuber, I can imagine how the residents of South Main Street in St. Albans felt the summer of 1926, when, knowing they'd grown some perfectly good "taters" because they'd actually harvested some, they ventured into their gardens to dig up a few potatoes for a poutine, potato salad or nice stew, only to find there were none.

The mounds they thought held the bounty of vegetables they had so lovingly tended were empty, which was quite a shock, because the theft was not immediately apparent. The cunning vegetable thieves had entered their gardens in the dark of night, pulled up the potato stalks, stolen all their potatoes and then reburied the plants so that the garden looked, to the casual eye, undisturbed.

To say the townspeople were outraged would be putting it mildly.

Chief of Police J.F. Mahoney was called to investigate. In his statement to the *Burlington Free Press*, he said that his men had their eyes peeled and that every effort would be made to capture the offender or offenders and bring them to justice. He also said that, until that time, the neighborhood had special dispensation to unleash their dogs to watch over their property.

The newspaper added that some residents, ready to go to the next level, had gotten out their shotguns to combat any more rounds of "spud thievery."

AHOY, SAILOR!

Late August 1930: Two sailors visiting Burlington on a long furlough took such a haphazard, high-speed joyride around the Queen City, calls from local residents caused police to suspect there might be at least twenty intoxicated drivers rampaging through all parts of town.

But motorcycle cops who were dispatched soon realized it wasn't a pack of drunken racers, just two boisterous young men with breath as fresh as the morning dew having a bit of fun before shipping out to sea. After receiving a good talking-to from the officers, the young men promised to leave the port city and head immediately to their waiting ship in Boston.

They drove away with their attitudes and driving skills much more subdued.

I COULD HAVE PREDICTED THAT

In the 1940s, listeners to radio station WCAX, which would eventually become WCAX-TV, were enthralled by a show called "Question and Problem Time" and the predictions of one Madame Zelaine. Zelaine, who also performed live for the Lions, Kiwanians, Rotarians and at larger events in Vermont, said she didn't rely on the use of crystals or other mystical tools and was not a "mind reader, fortune teller, or palmist"; rather, she had a sixth sense, a keenly tuned mind and a profound knowledge of human emotions.

Madame Zelaine forecast personal life events, but she also predicted events with global impact, like invasions and elections. She said her accuracy rate was 87 percent, a number that, like her predictions, seemed to come out of thin air. If only the famous seer had focused her consciousness on her own future, she might have been able to stop herself from being jailed for passing bad checks and being detained in the house of corrections in the summer of 1943.

Zelaine, who also went by the names Elaine Vance and Elaine Shanahan, gained a new name in the state of Vermont: "Madame Rubber Check."

THE MYSTERIOUS PANTY THIEF

In the town of Underhill in 1942, victims of a slippery criminal were growing sick and tired of a particular article of their clothing going missing.

Gathering up their wash at the end of the day, they discovered it devoid of one necessary item: their silk panties.

The "clothesline prowler," who was active from early summer and into fall, had stolen thirty-two pairs of the lustrous undergarments. Mrs. David Bentley, who had just purchased eight pairs for her young daughters, was so indignant at coming home to find them missing from her line that she went to her neighbors, teachers at the school situated across the street and the local sheriff to try to solve the crime.

The sheriff had his suspicions about who the thief might be, but there was no proof, and the crime remained unsolved. It was only after Mrs. Bentley made it known that she had written to WCAX radio personality and psychic Madame Zelaine to help locate them that the panties were eventually returned, wrapped in a brown paper bag and thrown anonymously into the Bentleys' yard.

WHO DOESN'T LOVE HOTDOGS?

One bright September morning in 1944, a stealthy young woman entered the home of Mr. and Mrs. Fred Fiske via a second-story window.

No, she wasn't some nimble arch-villain, only their "hired girl," Anna S. Warren of Riverside Avenue. Unknown to the Fiskes, she was planning to leave her job with them and figured she might as well take some souvenirs along with her. Warren, who'd been working in the Fiske home for just three weeks (with weekends off), entered the upstairs bedroom from the outside and, on the sly, took not just *her* clothes but those of others, including some nice dresses she'd been coveting.

Noting her absence the next day, the Fiskes discovered many personal possessions and even some silverware had gone missing. The items were later found, wrapped and waiting to be removed from the premises.

Warren, when questioned by police, revealed she'd decided to leave the job and needed the clothes because she hoped to secure work with a hot dog stand at the carnival. In court, she was ordered to spend four to six months in the house of corrections in Rutland.

Hot dog! *Library of Congress Archives.*

IMPERSONATING AN OFFICER

In 1948, a charlatan with a lot of nerve posed as an officer in order to accost a woman on Chase Street in Burlington.

Miss Annie Chin, a waitress of Chinese descent, said the man woke her out of a sound sleep and accused her of smuggling dope. He ordered her to get dressed and to go with him to police headquarters, saying her boyfriend was being held in connection with a local car theft.

Suspicious, Chin would not allow the interloper inside her house, deciding instead to do some investigating of her own. Making a quick phone call, she learned her boyfriend was not in jail.

She confronted the pretend police officer, who fled the scene in a taxicab. The quick-thinking Miss Chin memorized the cab's number and called police, who, in no time, found the driver. The cabbie told officers his fare had gotten out of the taxi and bolted on foot.

Patrols began a search for the imposter, who was apprehended and discovered to be Francis Tucker, thirty, of Charlotte, Vermont.

Tucker was cited into court, where he was found guilty of breaching the peace and impersonating an officer. He was fined twenty-five dollars and made to pay more than eight dollars in court costs.

It's possible that Tucker, previously part of the Army Transportation Corps port battalion, simply missed being in uniform.

22

THE LAST WOMAN

Mary Rogers of Hoosick Falls, New York, was an attractive girl—that, nobody could deny. With her dark, stormy eyes, jet-black hair and a creamy complexion, she had won over Marcus Rogers, a farmer more than ten years her senior, when she was merely a teen. Mary had grown up hard, with an alcoholic father who suffered from a mental illness, a situation she coped with by wandering. Marcus found her behavior unconventional, but he didn't seem to mind. They were eventually married, and he moved her to Shaftsbury, Vermont. In the spring of 1901, they had a child, Helen Alice Rogers. Six months later, Mary ran breathlessly to a neighbor's house, her face dripping tears. She told the neighbor she'd dropped baby Helen by accident. The neighbor, hurrying to check, found the infant near death from a fractured skull. Mary was the only witness. Police believed the bereaved mother's story, even though Marcus's relatives were convinced Mary had murdered the child.

Mary wasn't suited to motherhood, and she wasn't much suited to marriage. In fact, she had a reputation for being what people in those days called being a bit "sporty." When she and Marcus began to argue about money, which always seemed tight, Marcus decided they would move back to Hoosick Falls, where he would get a regular job. Mary declined.

Marcus left without her, and with her husband out of sight and out of mind, Mary was no longer feeling the need to be confined by her marriage vows. She began openly dating a man named Morris Knapp. Morris came from a family that was well respected and quite well off, both things Mary

Mary Rogers flanked by her husband, Marcus, and Leon Perham. *New England Historical Society.*

aspired to. She wanted to be married to him and figured where there was a will, there was a way, because unknown to Morris, Mary was also seeing two brothers, Levi and Leon Perham.

When Mary asked the Perham boys to help her kill her husband, Levi had the good sense to say *hell* no. But his younger brother, Leon, still a teenager whose sex-addled brain wasn't even fully formed yet, agreed with Mary's crazy plan.

Mary, pretending that she had an ongoing interest in her husband and their relationship, invited him to meet her in Bennington on August 9, 1902, at some picnic grounds near the Walloomsac River. Leon would be hiding nearby.

While catching up, Marcus told Mary he was upset about the local talk surrounding her sexual adventures with other men. Mary told him it was all just vicious rumors.

Drawing Marcus into her arms, Mary stroked his hair, entertaining him with a story of an evening a friend of hers had spent at the Rutland Opera House, where Henry Houdini, the great escape artist had been performing the most fascinating rope tricks. She wondered if Marcus would allow her to show him one. Marcus, besotted with her and way too trusting, agreed.

After she got his hands tied behind his back, Mary pressed a handkerchief loaded with chloroform over her husband's mouth and nose. Leon Perham jumped out of the bushes to assist. Despite the drug, there was quite a struggle. When all was said and done, Marcus was bruised, his ear nearly torn off and his skull crushed. Needless to say, he was a goner.

Mary lifted an envelope from her husband's coat, an insurance policy he kept there. She'd forged a suicide note and attached it to his hat. It said:

> *Blame no one, as I have at last put an end to my miserable life, as my wife knows I have threatened it....Everyone knows I have not anything or nobody to live for, and so blame no one as my last request, Marcus Rogers. Mary Rogers, I hope you will be happy.*

Mary lost no time in filing to collect her husband's insurance payout. In fact, she applied for it before there was even an autopsy. The police were keeping a suspicious eye on her and questioning her associates. It didn't take long for young Perham to spill the beans. At an inquest, unable to keep his part of the murder plot secret any longer, he told authorities everything. Prosecutors, feeling sorry for the seventeen-year-old, gave him a sentence of life in prison instead of execution.

But the prosecution did not spare Mary Rogers, painting her as a "cold, unwomanly monster."

When her mother visited her in prison, asking if she should send a priest to hear her confession, Mary replied, "You can take your priest and go to hell. I have no use for one."

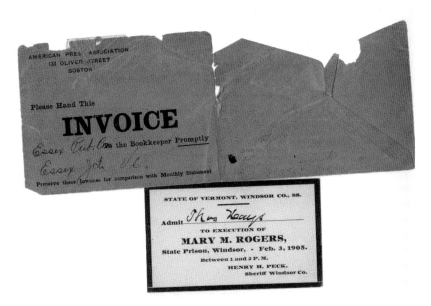

A ticket to the execution of Mary M. Rogers. *Digital Vermont: A Project of the Vermont Historical Society.*

On December 22, 1903, Rogers was found guilty and sentenced to death by hanging. The state's citizens were filled with horror and disbelief. Mary was a woman! She was only nineteen!

Previously, just one woman had been legally hanged in Vermont: Emeline Meaker, who, in 1883, poisoned a foster child with strychnine. For ten years, the state had commuted every death sentence they'd handed down. This time, with Mary, they were not so generous.

The public outcry went national. The case was appealed. Charles Bell, Vermont's governor at the time, received over forty thousand letters from around the country, asking him to spare Mary's life. Locked up in a cell at the prison in Windsor, Mary received thousands of letters, too. People sent gifts of food and candy. Mentally unstable and basking in her celebrity, she was far from contrite, and her bad behavior escalated. Conspiring with a prison matron, Mary managed to have sex with two different men, a convicted rapist and a prison guard. When questioned, the matron told authorities Mary had put her under a spell.

Fearing she was trying to get pregnant because she thought motherhood would sway public opinion, the warden decided the best place for Mary was solitary confinement. Still, her plan worked—almost. She gave birth to the nearly full-term child, but it was delivered stillborn.

On November 27, 1905, Governor Bell signed Mary's death warrant, setting the date of her execution for December 8, 1905. Thousands of letters asking him to reconsider didn't sway him.

On the morning of Mary's execution, Governor Bell met with her lawyers one last time, but he was tired of the entire affair. From the lawsuits to the public controversy, the woman and her case were making his life a living hell. His final word on the matter was, "I know of no law that is not as much for a woman as for a man."

On December 8, 1905, proving that, no matter the circumstances, Mary would be Mary, Rogers again intimated that she was pregnant. It didn't stall her death, which was even more horrifying than planned.

Mary walked to the scaffold and took off her glasses, handing them to the sheriff. A customary hood was pulled over her head, and the noose was placed around her neck. It was anticipated that the trapdoor would open and Mary's killing would be swift, but that wasn't what happened. The rope was too long, and Mary's feet hit the ground under the gallows. Witness gaped while the sheriff pulled her back up. Still, her neck did not break. The gallery stood for fourteen long minutes, watching the last woman to be executed in the state of Vermont slowly be strangled to death.

23

A LAST MEAL

There's a question I ask guests on my true crime tour that never fails to elicit nervous laughter: "If you were to commit a crime so heinous that you were locked up in prison and sentenced to death, what would your last meal be?"

Some people go all out: they want foie gras and thousand-dollar Papi steak, crab-stuffed squash blossoms drizzled with truffle oil and red wine–poached pears. Others say their favorite pizza or the perfect burger. One man said, "Just a bottle of good bourbon."

I always promise to tell them before the end of the tour about the last person who requested a last meal while they were a "guest" of our prison system here in Vermont.

I know his name, I know his crimes and I know what he ate.

Donald Demag was born in Burlington in 1922. By the time he was seventeen, he'd already caused enough trouble to land him in juvenile detention, but he first hit the papers as an adult criminal in 1946. Working as a truck driver, delivering goods, Demag saw a steel girder in a backyard on Bank Street in Burlington. The girder, which had been there for years, seemed like a good way to make a few bucks, so Demag took it. A couple of local policemen actually *saw* him take it, as it protruded quite a bit from the truck he was driving, but they thought nothing of it until its rightful owner, a Mrs. Meader Martin, complained. She wanted her girder back. But Demag no longer had it. He'd sold it for scrap. After Demag was cited into court, Judge Willsie Brisbin ordered him to pay the $9.90 he'd made to the salvage yard and return Mrs. Martin's girder posthaste. To teach him a lesson, the judge also gave him a day in the county jail.

Not long afterward, in 1947, Demag offended again and pleaded "nolo contender" to a hit-and-run charge and charges that he was using someone else's plates on his vehicle. The twenty-four-year-old was given a thirty-day sentence, suspended, with probation.

A year later, his pattern of committing small-time crimes became a thing of the past. On March, 14, 1948, he was picked up on North Street for the murder of a Burlington harness maker named Francis Racicot. Demag, who had an expectant wife and had been out of work for a few weeks, was friendly with the eighty-two-year-old and went into his shop, looking for a loan. Racicot, who had already loaned the young man thirty dollars, said no. An argument ensued, and Demag forced the much smaller man into the back of his shop, where he bludgeoned him with a heavy coal shaker from an old iron woodstove on the premises. He struck fifteen blows in all and then took Racicot's wallet and a coin purse containing less than $100. Had he checked, he would have found another $500 the harness maker had tucked in his vest.

Demag knew police were looking for Racicot's killer, but surprisingly, he didn't lie low. A few days after his violent act, he strolled past the harness shop and stood there for some time, just thinking. Then he went home and played

with his toddler, gave his wife, Virginia, a purse he'd bought for her downtown and took her to a dance. When they returned home, he confessed, saying police were looking for a man in a red coat, a wool plaid hunting jacket that was popular then and still is today. A witness saw a man of "stocky build" coming out of Racicot's shop wearing such a coat. Demag told Virginia he'd thrown the coat away and asked her to deny, if questioned, that he'd ever owned one.

A few days after Demag begged his wife to lie for him, the coat was found on a rooftop by a neighbor, who notified police.

Demag was captured and confessed to the murder, but prosecutors, fairly sure an insanity defense would be used, petitioned the court to have him evaluated at the Vermont State Hospital in Waterbury.

Donald Demag's booking photograph. *From the Burlington Daily News.*

146

When tested, Demag had an IQ of 88, categorized by experts in the field of measuring intelligence as being "below average." (His IQ would measure even lower after his incarceration.)

It was widely known that the young man had a temper, his short fuse possibly caused by his difficulty with communicating due to his almost total deafness, the result of scarlet fever, which he contracted as a toddler.

A childhood stay at the Austine School for the Deaf in Brattleboro, Vermont, was intended to help him overcome his language deficit, but until the 1960s, Austine was a "pure oral school." Only spoken and written English was used by instructors and students, with sign language not allowed until 1965. His frustration at the situation may have added to his feelings of isolation instead of alleviating them. Complicating matters was the fact Demag also had epilepsy, a neurological disorder that was stigmatized in those days and has also been known to affect well-being and social function. At his arraignment, Demag, who had confessed, ended up pleading not guilty, the plea made not by himself but by Judge Henry F. Black, who saw how close Clerk R.J Rousseau had to stand to the defendant in order for the profoundly deaf man to hear him.

On March 25, Demag was indicted by a grand jury and sent to the state hospital for his evaluation and a monthlong stay.

Finally, at trial in August 1948, his team wrangled a plea deal and a lesser charge, second-degree murder, bringing his trial to an end almost as soon as it began. Attorney General Clifton Parker accepted the plea, saying that while prosecutors felt Demag was sane when he killed Racicot, the defendant was known to have psychotic periods and, for the good of the public, should not be allowed in society. The judge deliberated for about fifteen minutes before accepting the plea, and he handed down a sentence of life in prison, to be served at the state prison in Windsor. Virginia Demag, who had just given birth to their second child a few weeks before, sat in the gallery with her father and other family members, crying softly as her husband was removed from the courtroom.

Just two years after being sent to Windsor, Demag left a dummy in his bed, just like they do in the movies, and managed a cunning escape.

Pretending to be sick for several days before he making a break for it, he tricked the guards, who believed he was absent from the exercise yard because he was asleep in his cell. While they rounded up prisoners and made bed checks, Demag was hiding in the shop where inmates made license plates. Guards on the wall left their posts after the final prisoner check, as usual. When the coast was clear, the athletically built felon hoisted himself over the sixteen-foot-tall prison wall with the aid of a long steel pole. His escape was not discovered until the following day. (Low IQ my eye.)

A BOLO, or "be on the lookout," order was issued to all law enforcement agencies. Police kept a sharp eye on the Burlington home of Demag's ex-wife, who had been granted a divorce after his incarceration. Powerful for his size and capable of "knocking a man down with a single blow," Demag was considered dangerous. Fifteen long days after his escape, Demag was picked up near the Canadian border in Newport.

A thirty-three-year-old border patrolman named J.J. Fell had just gotten off work when he saw Demag hitchhiking on the United States side of the border and stopped to give him a ride. Demag, now fitted with a hearing aid, told the patrolman he was from Canada, and Fell asked off-handedly if he'd remembered to report at the immigration office upon crossing the border. When Demag, who had actually gone over the border without detection but, for some reason, decided to re-enter Vermont, said no. Fell, having no idea who his passenger was, turned around and took him *back* to the border office. There, Demag lacked anything resembling a straight answer, and Fell, frustrated, asked him again where he was from. Demag said, "Burlington." The puzzled Fell wanted to know why the man changed his story. He warned Demag he'd better tell the truth or face jail, so Demag disclosed he was an escaped convict who was getting tired of his freedom. "Everyone is looking for me," he complained, saying he got "a funny feeling" every time he saw a police car. The Vermont State Police were notified, and an officer from the St. Johnsbury Barracks came to retrieve Demag. He was returned to prison, but it looked like he'd had finally found the thing he was good at: prison breaks. It wasn't long before he tried it again.

During the summer of 1952, at age twenty-nine, Demag, along with Francis Blair, thirty-one, of Middlebury, who was serving a two- to seven-year sentence for burglary, stole a ten-wheel heavy-duty work truck after prison employees left it unattended. They crashed it through the facility's heavy metal gates, pulling them off their hinges, and then they drove it at high speed through Windsor's residential area, abandoning it when it ran out of gas near Bellows Falls. Local papers described both men as "tough," but the five-foot-ten-inch-tall, 172-pound Demag was again described as "dangerous." It was noted that Demag and the more slightly built Blair weren't necessarily pals; rather, they were two guys who saw an opportunity to blow their crazy, court-mandated pop stand and just went with it.

Police scoured the woods and notified New Hampshire authorities of the breach. A posse led by bloodhounds was organized to search the

Francis Blair's booking photograph. *From the Burlington Daily News.*

area where the truck was found. The search for Demag and Blair was called the largest manhunt in Vermont history.

Wet, hungry and looking for less conspicuous clothing while on the run and bushwhacking through forests, the pair happened upon the Springfield, Vermont home of Elizabeth Weatherup and her husband, Donald.

Mrs. Weatherup, who'd attended a civil defense meeting earlier in the evening, arrived home after her husband went to bed. At about 12:30 a.m., she woke him, saying she'd heard noises outside their front door. Thinking it was the family dog, Donald got up to check. Just outside the door, he was hit with an iron pipe. While grappling with the intruders, he heard his wife scream and was hit again, after which he fell unconscious. He never saw his attackers, who left him for dead and entered his home.

The two men found Elizabeth hiding in the bathroom. She was bludgeoned by Blair and stabbed with the tang end of a large file carried by Demag. Officer Lashua, a Springfield cop who responded to the scene, said the retired schoolteacher was found sitting on the floor, her head on the bathtub and blood flowing into the tub and down the drain. She was transported to the local hospital, where doctors observed 680 cracks in her bones and skull.

At some point during the attack, Donald, who was bleeding profusely (it would later be discovered he had three scalp wounds, ten or twelve puncture wounds and a fractured rib and right wrist), regained consciousness and managed to get to his neighbor's house to call for help. It didn't take long before the area was crawling with cops from units all over the state. Hastily set up roadblocks plugged the streets for miles.

Bloodhounds on the scene pointed the way to a place called the Bishop farm, where a Springfield man named Francis Plumb opened fire on the two escapees. Demag split off and ran into the woods while Plumb held Blair at gunpoint.

It was St. Albans state trooper Marvin Pfenning who finally nabbed Demag, running him down until the culprit finally turned around and surrendered, his shirt spattered with Elizabeth Weatherup's blood. Both criminals, wearing coats and pants with Mr. Weatherup's name on them, were taken to the Springfield Police Station. Found in their possession were other articles taken from the victims' home, including Mrs. Weatherup's purse, which contained forty-seven dollars and some change.

Francis Blair was the first to be tried. Unsurprisingly, he was sentenced to death by electrocution. Before he died on February 8, 1954, Blair played checkers with the prison's Catholic chaplain Reverend William Ready. Earlier, he had written a letter stating Mrs. Weatherup had been a nice woman and that he was actually the one responsible for her murder. He asked that Demag be spared.

That didn't happen. Demag's trial was filled with expected delays. One humorous piece of information the public got came via the police officers who were responsible for guarding him as the hearings were ongoing. It seems being on the hook for murder didn't ruin his appetite. During just one lunch they supervised, the defendant ate an order of soup, French fries, mashed potatoes, a steak, a pie à la mode, a western sandwich and then even more pie.

Eventually, Demag's time and his gargantuan lunches ran out. He was found guilty and was scheduled to be executed at the prison in Windsor on December 8, 1954. His last meal was not extravagant: two pork chops, a baked potato, chocolate cake and chocolate ice cream.

The execution room, lit by a single naked bulb, was empty except for the electric chair and the device the executioner would use to flip the switch. At Blair's execution, even though it was believed he, the more psychopathic and violent of the two, had actually killed Elizabeth Weatherup, there were only two guards in attendance. Demag's execution was a different story. The physically imposing man, known to be impulsive and quick-tempered, had nearly a dozen guards and prison officials to keep him in line.

Sedated, with his hearing aid removed and his face completely covered by a mask, Demag entered the room with the prison chaplain. The executioner, who remained anonymous, was dressed respectfully as befit the occasion in a nondescript suit and tie. Guards strapped Demag into the chair, and as his body was prepared for what was to come. The chaplain offered prayers, with Demag finally joining him in the Lord's Prayer. At the line "deliver us from evil," the executioner pulled the switch. When it was over, the prison doctor, Dr. William Krause, pulled out his stethoscope to have a listen and verified Donald Demag was dead.

Demag was the last Vermonter to be executed in that manner, as death by electrocution was deemed "cruel and unusual punishment." If you're as curious as many of my tour guests, you might wonder what happened to the old electric chair.

An example of a standard-issue electric chair. *Wikipedia.*

Vermont's electric chair is hidden away in the basement of the Vermont Historical Society in Barre. The artifact from a more barbaric time lives in a climate-controlled basement. The storage area that holds it is home to various pieces of antique furniture—but perhaps none quite so interesting or so ghoulish. It spends its time under a sheet so it won't upset people who might come upon it accidentally. Under the terms of the deal that bestowed the chair to the society, it can't be put on public display, so it's rarely seen— and hardly ever discussed.

BIBLIOGRAPHY

Associated Press. "Durenleau Appeals to Vermont Hight Court." *Burlington Free Press*, May 12, 1994.

———. "Woman Pleads Innocent in Drug Dealer's Killing." *Rutland Herald*, August 12, 2004.

Bartlett, Ellen, and Jane Smith. "Colchester Woman Dead in Shooting." *Burlington Free Press*, May 6, 1978.

Beerworth, Jeffrey H. *Historic Crimes and Justice in Burlington, Vermont.* Charleston, SC: The History Press, 2015.

Biography.com. "Ted Bundy." April 3, 2013. https://www.biography.com/crime/ted-bundy.

Braun, William H. "Fatal Shooting Inquest 'Disappointing.'" *Burlington Free Press*, January 6th, 1981

Burlington Clipper. "Fatally Stabbed During a Drunken Orgie on Battery Street." May 5, 1881.

———. "More Injunctions for Selling Liquor." June 22, 1901.

———. "Philomene Lemoine, Grand Jury." September 27, 1888.

Burlington Daily News. "City News, Philomene Lemoine." April 23, 1880.

———. "Court to Rule on Admissibility of Deathbed Statement." January 12, 1937.

———. "Repudiation Is Denied by DeShaw." March 15, 1948.

———. "Sailor's Joy Ride Broken Up by Police." August 28, 1930.

Burlington Democrat. "William Carbo Charged." November 9, 1871.

Burlington Free Press. "Admits Taking Dress." September 11, 1944.

———. "Barbershop Yields Some Alleged Beer." August 20, 1928.

———. "Beatrice Heed Asks for Divorce." August 13, 1926.

———. "Church Street Store Scene of Attempted Murder and Suicide." March 3, 1926.

———. "Community News, Heed-Rubado Nuptials." March 22, 1947.

———. "Court Docket, Philomene Lemoine." April 23, 1880.

———. "Court Docket, Philomene Pasha, Sale of Russell House." July 22, 1910.

———. "Day in Court, Ellen Ducharme." June 6, 1985; July 2, 1985; November 6, 1985; December 18, 1985; March 15, 1986; March 21, 1986; May 31, 1986; January 1, 1987; February 24, 1987; October 1, 1987; November 26, 1987; March 4, 1988; November 2, 1988; July 22, 1989; March 26, 1992; September 16, 1992; January 25, 1993; October 12, 1995; April 17, 1999; February 2, 2000.

———. "Diary: Accused Murderer Vowed to Kill." June 2, 1987.

———. "Did No Wrong, Magee Says at His Hearing." May 3, 1962.

———. "Donald DeMag, Burlington Doing a Life Term for Murder Succeeds in Escaping from Windsor Prison." August 28, 1950.

———. "Donald DeMag, Two Time Murderer Electrocuted." December 9, 1954.

———. "Don't Know Why Asserts Malloy." December 22, 1961.

———. "Ernest Rubado Arrested, Vergennes." July 15, 1930.

———. "Eva LaCourse Dies Three Days After Shooting" May 20, 1936.

———. "Heed May leave Hospital This Week." March 8, 1926.

———. "Jail Instead of Altar." October 23, 1919.

———. "Local Girl Victim, Former Sweetheart Turns Gun on Self." May 16, 1933.

———. "Local Woman Is Made Defendant in $5,000 Suit." November 8, 1933.

———. "Man Who Posed as Policeman Gets $25 Fine." June 26, 1948.

———. "Maurice Poulin…Hangs Self in Windsor Prison." September 11, 1944.

———. "Mrs. Lemoine Burned Out." October 28, 1881.

———. "Murder Suspect Changes Plea." June 17, 1978.

———. "Mystery Surrounds Panties Theft." November 10, 1942.

———. "Needed Money Declares Adams." December 22, 1961.

———. Obituary, Ligia Collins. August 5, 2004.

———. Obituary, Michael Durenleau. July 19, 1985.

———. "Papers Served, George Cathey." July 23, 1908.

———. "Poulin Indicted by Grand Jury." September 17, 1936.

———. "State Says Mrs. Weatherup Slain with Iron Pipe and File." December 9, 1953.

———. "Teenager Put on Probation for Knife Threat." April 9, 1981.

———. "Thief Arrested/William Corbo." March 18, 1881. https://www.newspapers.com/image/145522522/?terms=William%20Corbo&match=1.

———. "Three More City Policemen Charged with Theft on Duty." January 13, 1962.

CBS NEWS. "Solving the Murders of Israel Keyes." https://www.cbsnews.com/pictures/solving-israel-keyes-murders/.

"Court Reveals Daughter's Death Attempt." *Vidette* 91, no. 43 (September 29, 1978): 8. Milner Library.

Criminal Genealogy. "John Larney, AKA Mollie Matches." https://criminalgenealogy.blogspot.com/2020/01/john-larney-aka-mollie-matches-con-man.html.

Curran, John. "Life in Prison for Murder of UVM Student." *Bennington Banner*, October 18, 2006.

Daily Free Press and Times. "Mercier in Court." May 10, 1881.

———. "Murder." May 2, 1881.

———. "(Police Blotter) William Corbo." March 15, 1881.

———. "Shocking Homicide on Water Street." October 27, 1871.

Donlan, Ann E. "Convict Denies Role in Husband's Murder." *Burlington Free Press*, March 23, 1993.

Donoghue, Mike. "Affidavit Outlines Plot After Killing." *Burlington Free Press*, April 22, 1992.

———. "Body of Colchester Woman Found." *Burlington Free Press*, March 10, 1998.

———. "Colchester Man Charged with Killing His Wife." *Burlington Free Press*, March 20, 1998.

———. "Deadly Silence." *Burlington Free Press*, March 29, 1998.

———. "Defense Seeks Retrial in Murder Case." *Burlington Free Press*, October 22, 1992.

———. "Durenleau Guilty in Slaying." *Burlington Free Press*, August 31, 1992.

———. "Elder Hamlin Arraigned." *Burlington Free Press*, June 6, 1981.

———. "Essex Police Search Missing Couple's House." *Burlington Free Press*, June 10, 2011.

———. "Expert: Two Attacked Victim." *Burlington Free Press*, August 26, 1992.

———. "Franklin Woman Denies Part in Slaying." *Burlington Free Press*, September 14, 1991.

———. "High Court Frees Woman." *Burlington Free Press*, October 1, 1994.

———. "Inmate Can't Attend Wedding." *Burlington Free Press*, July 27, 1994.

———. "Inmate Seeks Permission to Attend Daughter's Wedding." *Burlington Free Press*, July 26, 1994.

———. "Jury Begins Deliberations." *Burlington Free Press*, August 30, 1992.

———. "1985 Killing Goes to Trial." *Burlington Free Press*, August 25, 1992.

———. "Police Pursue Lead in Case of Missing Couple." *Burlington Free Press*, February 8, 2012.

———. "Police Seize Belongings of Dead Woman." *Burlington Free Press*, March 11, 1998.

———. "Wife Charged with Aiding 1985 Killing." *Burlington Free Press*, September 13, 1991.

———. "Woman in Slaying Case Is Released." *Burlington Free Press*, September 20, 1991.

Donoghue, Mike, and Adam Silverman. "Serial Killer's Suicide Brings End to Currier Case." *Burlington Free Press*, December 3, 2012.

Federal Bureau of Investigation. "Israel Keyes Interviews." YouTube. https://www.youtube.comwatch?v=C-Yx0i3qOfQ&t=2432s.

———. "Serial Murder." https://www.fbi.gov/stats-services/publications/serial-murder.

FindLaw. "State of Vermont vs. Herman L. Yoh." https://caselaw.findlaw.com/vt-supreme-court/1344939.html.

Gentler, Gayle. "Woman Sent to Jail in Daughter's Death." *Burlington Free Press*, December 31, 1978.

Heany, Joe. "Two Policemen Get Prison Sentences." *Burlington Free Press*, March 13, 1962.

Heller, Paul. "The Hanging of Mary Rogers." *Barre-Montpelier Times Argus*, August 2, 2019. https://www.timesargus.com/news/local/the-hanging-of-mary-rogers/article_f126f464-484b-56ab-90ae-77399208692a.html.

Hubbard, Amy. "Alleged Serial Killer Found Dead But Closure Eludes Some Families." *Los Angeles Times*, December 3, 2012. https://www.latimes.com/nation/la-xpm-2012-dec-03-la-na-nn-israel-keyes-suspect-serial-killer-20121203-story.html.

Johnson, Mark. "Police Have Suspect in Essex Murder Case." *Burlington Free Press*, July 19, 1985.

———. "Police Still Hunting Clues in Stabbing of Swanton Man." *Burlington Free Press*, July 17, 1985.

———. "Wright's Link to Second Killing Difficult to Prove." *Burlington Free Press*, December 25, 1986.

Johnson, Mark, and Danica Kirka. "Suspect Arrested in Double Murder." *Burlington Free Press*, December 6, 1986.

Johnson, Tim. "Gardner Quinn Praised for Ability to Connect with People, Nature." *Burlington Free Press*, October 16, 2006.

Just U.S. Law. "In re: Ellen Ducharme." https://law.justia.com/cases/vermont/superior-court/2012/s0319-10-cncv.html.

Larsen, Erik. *The Devil in the White City*. New York: Knopf Doubleday Publishing Group, 2003.

Leagle. "State V. Wright." Supreme Court of Vermont, November 17, 1989. https://www.leagle.com/decision/19891301581a2d72011299#.

Lippman, John. "Vermont Historical Society Stores Windsor State Prison's Electric Chair." *Valley News*, August 9, 2017. https://www.vnews.com/Vermont-s-electric-chair-hidden-in-Barre-11676974.

Low, Kylie. "Rita Curran: Solving Vermont's Oldest Cold Case, Parts 1&2." Dark Downeast. https://www.darkdowneast.com/episodes/ritacurran.

Lush, Tamara. "Yoh Guilty of Wife's Murder." *Burlington Free Press*, October 19, 1999.

Maerki, Vic. "Heard Larceny Report on Police in July, Bing Says." *Burlington Free Press*, May 4, 1962.

Mahoney, Joe. "Suspects Called Both Quiet, Tempestuous." *Burlington Free Press*, May 22, 1981.

"Mary Rogers Ready to Die." *San Francisco Call* 97, no. 61 (January 30, 1905): 3.

Meyer, Peter. *Death of Innocence*. New York: G.P. Putnam's Sons, April 1985.

Murderpedia. "Mary Mable Rogers." https://murderpedia.org/female.R/r/rogers-mary-mabel.htm.

New England Historical Society. "Mary Rogers Brings the Capital Punishment Wars to Vermont." November 8, 1933. https://newenglandhistoricalsociety.com/mary-rogers-brings-the-capital-punishment-wars-to-vermont/.

O'Shea, Kathleen A. *Women and the Death Penalty in the United States*. Westport, CT: Praeger Publishers, 1999.

Page, Candace. "Search Goes On for Missing Essex Couple." *Burlington Free Press*, June 12, 2011.

Peck, Jodie. "Brookes Ave Woman was Shot in Head." *Burlington Free Press*, January 5, 1981.

———. "Mother Found Slain in Front of Her Home." *Burlington Free Press*, January 4, 1981.

Perron, Darren. "Reporter's Notebook: Remembering the Murder Case That Changed Vermont." WCAX-TV. June 11, 2021. https://www.wcax.com/2021/06/11/reporters-notebook-remembering-murder-case-that-changed-vermont/.

Picard, Ken. "U.S. Attorney Coffin: Currier Couple 'Fought to the End' Against 'a Force of Pure Evil.'" *Seven Days*, December 3, 2012. https://www.sevendaysvt.com/OffMessage/archives/2012/12/03/us-attorney-coffin-currier-couple-fought-to-the-end-against-a-force-of-pure-evil.

Polumbaum, Ian. "Defense Rests Case in Wright Trial." *Burlington Free Press*, January 13, 1988.

———. "Defense to Put Samuel Wright Jr. on Stand." *Burlington Free Press*, January 10, 1988.

———. "Jury Finds Wright Guilty." *Burlington Free Press*, January 14, 1988.

———. "Victim's Father Testifies in Samuel Wright Trial." *Burlington Free Press*, January 7, 1988.

Reilly, John. "Woman Admits Killing Her Daughter." *Burlington Free Press*, September 28, 1978.

Rule, Ann. *The Stranger Beside Me*. W.W. New York: Norton & Company, August 1980.

Ryan, Matt. "Essex Police Widen the Net." *Burlington Free Press*, August 5, 2011.

Schecter, Harold. *Depraved*. New York: Pocket Books, 1994.

Sikes, Gina. "The Murder of a Beautiful Girl." *Cosmopolitan*, February 2007.

Silverman, Adam. "Investigators Examine Home in Richmond; Parents Issue Plea for Help." *Burlington Free Press*, October 11, 2006.

———. "Israel Keyes: I'm Two Different People." *Burlington Free Press*, December 4, 2012.

———. "Killer Must Wait to learn Sentence." *Burlington Free Press*, November 29, 2006.

———. "Police Name Third Suspect in Collins Slaying." *Burlington Free Press*, August 3, 2004.

———. "Rooney Charged in Student's Death." *Burlington Free Press*, October 26, 2006.

———. "Student's Disappearance 'Suspicious.'" *Burlington Free Press*, October 9, 2006.

———. "Suspects ID'd in Woman's Death." *Burlington Free Press*, July 14, 2004.

State of Vermont. "Unsolved Homicides. Department of Public Safety, Vermont State Police. https://vsp.vermont.gov/unsolved.

Theriault Boots, Michelle. "The Untold Story Behind Israel Keyes' Jailhouse Suicide." *Anchorage Daily News*, July 15, 2014. https://www.adn.com/alaska-news/article/untold-story-behind-israel-keyes-jailhouse-suicide/2014/07/15/.

True Crime Diva. "Who Killed Vermont Mother of Three Angela Louise Belisle in 1981?" July 12, 2022. https://truecrimediva.com/angela-louise-belisle/.

True Crime New England. "Episode 22: Donald Demag." https://www.truecrimene.com/episodes/6z2e8yfv4iwre1a8tuj302xvzfor2p.

Vermont Cynic. "Michelle Gardner Quinn Case Closed." September 2, 2008. https://vtcynic.com/news/michelle-gardner-quinn-case-closed/.

Vermont in the Civil War. "Israel Freeman." http://vermontcivilwar.org/get.php?input=39033.

Vermont Superior Court Civil Division. "Herman Yoh vs. James Baker-CIVIL DIVISION Case No. 21-CV-01699." Judiciary of Vermont. https://www.vermontjudiciary.org.

v|lex. "STATE of Vermont v. Herman L. Yoh, No. 00-160. No. 05-083." Supreme Court of Vermont. https://case-law.vlex.com/vid/state-v-yoh-no-889873930.

Walsh, Molly. "Questions, Few Answers for Relatives, Co-Workers." *Burlington Free Press*, June 11, 2011.

WCAX-TV. "Rita Curran Case Closed." February 22, 2023. https://www.wcax.com/video/2023/02/22/rita-curran-case-closed-cigarette-butt-leads-police-killer-1971-burlington-murder/.

Wikipedia. "Donald DeMag." https://en.wikipedia.org/wiki/Donald_DeMag.

———. "Israel Keyes." https://en.wikipedia.org/wiki/Israel_Keyes.

———. "Michelle Gardner-Quinn." https://en.wikipedia.org/wiki Murder_of_Michelle_Gardner-Quinn.

Wild, Kendall. "Present at the Execution." *Rutland Herald*, July 20, 2005.

Woollaston, Victoria. "How to Spot a Serial Killer: Criminologists Reveal Five Key Traits." DailyMail.UK, MailOnline, July 21, 2015. https://www.dailymail.co.uk/sciencetech/article-3169359/How-spot-serial-killer-Criminologists-reveal-five-key-traits-common-notorious-murderers.html.

Youngwood, Susan. "Swanton Man, 35, Dies After Stabbing in Essex." *Burlington Free Press*, July 14, 1985.

ABOUT THE AUTHOR

Thea Lewis is a best-selling Vermont author and the owner of Queen City Entertainment, the umbrella company for her True Crime Burlington and Queen City Ghostwalk tours. She's been featured in publications like *Yankee Magazine*, the *Hartford Courant* and *Vermont Magazine* and has appeared on the CW television network, along with numerous other programs and podcasts originating in the United States and Canada.

This is her sixth book with The History Press.